WHY DID YOU GIVE UP THE *KOOCHIE* AND NOW YOU MAD

Understanding God's Idea of
Woman, Wife, and Marriage

Shadoew Rose Terrell

BALBOA.
PRESS

A DIVISION OF HAY HOUSE

ISBN: 978-1-4525-6002-1 (sc)
ISBN: 978-1-4525-6003-8 (e)
ISBN: 978-1-4525-6004-5 (hc)

Library of Congress Control Number: 2012918660

Balboa Press books may be ordered through booksellers or by contacting:

Balboa Press
A Division of Hay House
1663 Liberty Drive
Bloomington, IN 47403
www.balboapress.com
1-(877) 407-4847

Because of the dynamic nature of the Internet, any web addresses or links contained in this book may have changed since publication and may no longer be valid. The views expressed in this work are solely those of the author and do not necessarily reflect the views of the publisher, and the publisher hereby disclaims any responsibility for them.

The author of this book does not dispense medical advice or prescribe the use of any technique as a form of treatment for physical, emotional, or medical problems without the advice of a physician, either directly or indirectly. The intent of the author is only to offer information of a general nature to help you in your quest for emotional and spiritual well-being. In the event you use any of the information in this book for yourself, which is your constitutional right, the author and the publisher assume no responsibility for your actions.

Any people depicted in stock imagery provided by Thinkstock are models, and such images are being used for illustrative purposes only.
Certain stock imagery © Thinkstock.

Printed in the United States of America

Balboa Press rev. date: 11/21/2012

Dedication

I dedicate this book to women who have never known God's idea of them. So often, we make terrible mistakes, because we do not know whom we are. We adhere to an idea of what someone else told us, ideas, not necessarily accurate, nor esteemed by God's concept of us.

Some suggest it is an old, or antiquated way of thinking; turning and acknowledging the thoughts of the One who built and fashioned women with delicacy and intricacy. His ideas are still relevant. They are relevant, because, every day we rise to discover His idea toward us the more. When we learn more about ourselves according to His Word, which empowers us to defend ourselves with His mind. We no longer accept anything, but rather, elevate our conscious to greater concepts and a higher order of thought for our lives. No an order established according to the minds of men. Rather, an order established and sanctioned by the One who built us, as a complement to man. My earnest desire is for women to look at God's idea regarding her.

To God do I give honor and glory. I did not intend to write what is written when I first began. It has become a very different book in terms of its dialogue. God lead me through endless hours of research. Nine years later, this is what I believe He produced. As time progressed, I learned I was not just writing another book. I was writing for the broken in spirit. I was writing for women who could not identify their value. I was writing for women who lost their self worth, and self-esteem.

I write for the silent. I write for the abused. I write for those whose heartache continues. I write with the intent of women healing from sadness and sickness of soul. I write in hopes of a woman's spirit being renewed. I write in hopes of women learning God's definition of who they are, and women understanding what God said about love, their care, and treatment.

God knows and He sees. He hears a woman's cries when no one else hears her crying. He will comfort her when no one knows she needs comforting. He recognizes every woman, and counts her so precious and valuable. Women are significant and important to God. They are the apple of His eye. I hope women learn of how important they are to Him. Woman, you are precious in the eyes of God.

The experiences and words in this work are to build women in the knowledge of God's idea of woman, wife, and marriage, as well as enlighten men in God's intended care for her.

Table of Contents

Acknowledgements

None of this would be possible without my beautiful husband, Clarence. I thank him for being my man, husband, and my best friend. I with all sincerity appreciate the beauty of God's Spirit within him. He is God's expression of love for me. A gift God graced me to happily receive.

Clair, you are the priest and prophet of our home. Thank you for your prayers and Godly counsel. I appreciate your leadership and direction. Thank you for always directing me to consult with the One who enables me to do all things-Christ. With all my heart, I love you.

You have come home to stumble over numerous articles: research materials; commentaries; bibles; and whatever else encircled me, as I sat studying on our bedroom floor. I thank you for your corrections, and input. You know how I love sitting under you, listening to your wisdom, and sound counsel.

You missed a few dinners as I engrossed myself in this work. I must say, "Thank you baby, for your patience, care, and endless support." Thank you for all the moments you thought, I worked too much. For the moments, you stopped me to break for Ice Cream, and the many moments you pulled me away to grab a bite to eat. Thank you for all the times I worked from sunup to sunset. Without noticing night had fallen; you came in and turned the light on for me. You are my hero.

Ms. Johnnie, I thank you for committing your daughter to God, and teaching her about life in Christ. I did not always follow those instructions. Yet, I never forgot them. However, what Scripture teaches speaks truth. "Train a child in the way in which they should go, and in the latter days they shall follow." Thank God for the promise of His Word. I rest safely in His arms. Thank you Mom…I love you.

I thank all my siblings for their support in my endeavors. I appreciate the comments, suggestions, and criticism. I have learned invaluable wisdom and knowledge from all of you. Because of your individual contributions, I stand on all your shoulders. Continue your pursuit of God. As you know, God pursued all of you from the beginning. You have always been His.

There is one other person I need to acknowledge, Charnell. Thank you for the other pair of eyes, catching what I missed. Thank you for your dedication, time, and heartfelt comments. I appreciate you.

Introduction

Several years ago, my sister and I were eating breakfast at my Mom's home in Northern California. We began a casual conversation about us as women, and why we act the way, we sometimes do. What started the conversation was a mutual friend's predicament with an ex-girlfriend. He decided to sever their involvement, but agreed to the mutual care of their child. Angered by his decision to dissolve their intimate relations, she emptied his fully furnished home. However, after court proceedings, he recovered most of his belongings.

We laughed as we elaborated on the madness we experienced in our own lives. Although we expressed amusement, we realized madness was not a comical matter. Especially, after reflecting upon the women we knew and the madness they endured through heartache. Some misfortune appeared self-inflicted, while other broken hearts resulted from deception.

His circumstances provoked us to engage in a deeper assessment of the various difficulties us as women allow. As well as the madness associated with decisions consequent to our choices. Choices, we make, and find ourselves in unhealthy affairs, which damage both heart and soul. Yet, despite truth, we struggle to remove self from the madness we discover. Madness not necessarily defined as anger. Rather, madness defined as a condition of brokenness, and sadness of soul. Madness based on decisions made against our own well-being, and choosing to remain in the chaos.

Why as women do we decide against changing our predicament when we hold the power to do so? Why do we repeatedly reach for a glimmer of light to suggest, "Everything will be wonderful?" Why do we commit to what we know is not good for us? Why do we work against self?

I have discovered many of us embrace hope, desiring a loving relation. We surrender our hearts, bodies, and souls as a down payment to secure our want. We anticipate with expectancy, as we look forward to our return on investment. We cleave to optimism, and trust our love will draw the return of something fulfilling and satisfying. We allow the influence of our heart to believe, because we love, exchange will occur.

Therefore, we hold to an idea while we ignore the knock on our conscience, which begs to disagree. We neglect the tap on the mind and prefer to chase what the heart yearns. We surrender both body and soul, often to our grief, and find ourselves in a state of madness. Madness not based on anger, but madness because of broken heartedness; madness because of dissatisfaction and sadness of soul.

Women want to create a pleasant atmosphere by giving herself in love. She will diligently work to create a harmonious environment. Even if she knows, the man does not share her sentiments. If she allows her heart to yearn and deny the differences, time will tick away, and the truth will reveal itself to agree with what she suppressed. What she held down will eventually rise to the surface, she will face what she denied.

In conclusion, she will find her passions drained and her mind exhausted. Weighed with sadness as she realizes what she longed-for, did not occur. What she invested is hopeless. Her time, energy, and passion she expelled wasted; however, the lesson learned priceless. What she spent must count as a loss. Despite it all, she must recover the love she gave; apply it to self, to heal the pain.

As our conversation continued, questions developed regarding why women think they are in need of the opposite sex. Scripture teaches God created the woman for the man, not the man for the woman. God after creating man identified his need and fashioned woman as his assistant. God did not create the man as woman's help. He fashioned woman as a contributor to further man in his effort and purpose in life. God created woman as man's complement. Many women do not understand the importance of her role. Therefore, many run after a misconception, instead of pacing alongside God's truth.

Scripture teaches a *man* finds a 'good thing.' He is the aggressor who seeks. He ought to be searching for… Today women are on the prowl to chase and snag what they can. Women compromise God's order, as they exchange the truth for want. Young and old both declare, 'I am not waiting on a man to discover me. I will go find one.' Does this have a familiar sound? If you did not say it, or think it, perhaps you heard it from one of your friends. Such a disposition will lead to major disappointments, as well as heartache.

If a woman believes she can transform the heart of any man she has chosen; she deceives her own heart. Her pursuit to catch him is unnatural. She places herself in a position to calculate how she will win him, and keep figuring out how to keep her prize. She must continue to calculate because she can never feel secure and safe in his heart, knowing she lured and snagged him. She finds herself suspicious and questioning his intentions. If he sought and wooed her, she knows he chased her heart only to capture his.

How many women regret her chase, discovering she could not compel her man's heart to fall into hers? It mattered not about her job title; gifts, or koochie; nor the children she intentionally birth, to win him over. However, through her heartache, she learns, after all she has done, she could not turn his heart. The grievous disappointment gnaws at her soul. Her madness begins, when truth collides with lies told to her own heart, and the lies become magnified.

More Madness

Men, who harass the heart of women without any intent to surrender his heart for her capture, produce another element of madness; a madness that develops in false hope. These types of men stimulate dishonest ideas. They sell the thought of possibility with Stellar performances. A despairing game played at the cost of a woman's heart, and at the expense of a woman's soul. A man who feeds a woman's heart with illusions of hope is dishonest. He fuels her soul with false emotions evoking her to want what he knows he will never surrender-himself. He plays for sheer self-gratification, emotionally devastating another, without regret. Toying with a person's soul is cruel, and the worst form of deception. It is deceitfulness beautifully packaged and wrapped in lies.

Women have emotional depth and intellectual insight. However, too often, women disconnect from God's wisdom, or intuition to follow their own emotions. Emotions are not always accurate, and should never out weight intellect. How often have we neglected conscious for feelings, and found ourselves compromised? God gave women brilliant minds; even so, when it comes to men; emotions control the psyche.

A woman's greatest difficulty is often her self-esteem. Often she does not recognize her significance, nor is she aware of her relevance. Women face this all the time. They look for a male figure to confirm and approve their importance, instead of seeing themselves for whom they are. Why do women believe they need approval, when God Himself approved and created their significance and importance? You would think this would be enough, but it is not.

Depending on every woman's faith in herself, it will decide her confidence, and self-esteem. If she discovers who she is, and confident in her findings, she is more secure in her decision-making process. Then again, I have seen assured women make unfavorable choices about men; especially, when the volume of their heart deafens the voice of reason in their mind.

If her self-esteem is low, and she struggles with confidence, she may accept what she should never embrace, as well as refuse what she believes she does not deserve. A woman must know and believe the significance God placed in her, and embrace the reality of God sanctioning her worth.

Is the Question Still Relevant?

Although we spoke about this issue many years ago, the subject, "Why did you give up the koochie and now you mad," remains a relevant discussion for conversation today. As I look from my youth, until now, women still surrender everything. I have seen family members, friends, friend's families, and co-workers, give all to their own hurt. How do women lessen the madness and stop self-inflicting? "We as women must come into a true knowledge of God's idea of woman, wife, and marriage."

A woman should know what Scripture's declares about her. It is essential she understand God's mind toward her, and the treatment God ordained for her life. God created within women a fervent want for love. He also gave man the details on how to satisfy her want. He declares to man; love her as Christ loves His body-the Church. Christ woos with passion, romance, and intimacy, so should a husband. God's marital plan describes His cherished desire for romance, and His expression exercised in relations between man and woman.

When a man recognizes, he found a *'good thing,'* he will pour everything into her God determined in his heart. What God commanded the husband to yield will satisfy her desires. Her reception in his heart will be to her delight. God commanded the husband to love his wife in a particular way, and gave him specific instruction on how to carry out those directives. If he gives as God taught, he will not only satisfy, but also quench what she thirsts. For God placed in man a passionate love for the woman…he finds to wife.

What began as a question later became the basis to develop a read for men and women to grasp God's mind. We need to understand and examine God's thoughts for women, as well as men in marriage. Women can learn and discover their incredible and remarkable assets and abilities, and the honor bestowed upon them by God. Men can understand God's expectations, and the honorable responsibility God charged them with for the care and treatment of their complements.

The Work and Intent

This work begins with forgiveness. It touches on strong subject matters relating to some Christian struggles. It discusses a woman's influence. The inherent ability women possess to stimulate a man's emotions. Those qualities gifted from God belong to her husband, not Tom, Dick, or Harry. It concludes with defining the Scriptural meaning of marriage. You may find some chapters strong and direct. The discussions are necessary because they exist.

It is my hope we who claim Christianity will consider Scriptural truth, and align self-with God's idea. Thus, encouraging God's children to manage their conduct as God intended. The reader must examine the context with an open mind, as some subject matters will challenge traditional teachings.

For those who may read this work who are not Christian, consider the mind of God, and His thoughts of you and toward you. Upon evaluating His love, determine for yourself, which is better, His ideas, or the traditions of men.

This book will motivate every reader to take a fresh look at Scriptural ideas referencing marital relations. If your heart is open to truth, it will challenge you to consider your conduct towards your spouse. Overall, when you finish, I hope you close this book with a different perspective about your complement. I hope respect and honor for husband and wife revives, and the heart explodes with fresh passion. More than anything study and search the Scriptures for you.

Fasten your seat belts; this work will take you through mountains and valleys. Do not be faint at heart. It is serious content. Content that happens in the lives of men and women every day. This is a small platform to open these concerns for conversation. However, they are necessary. These issues may be of concern to you, or your acquaintances. Keep in mind this work is for growth: maturity; instruction; inspiration, and purposed to free you in the Word of God.

Delayed With Cause

For several years, I set this book aside as I sought the counsel of God to understand His idea of the marital union between husband and wife. Since my husband and I had become marriage coaches, I needed to understand God's mind as a woman and wife for myself. Not based on what I thought, but established on what God said.

I noted information as God opened my mind to understand His ideas about holy matrimony. Besides the previously mentioned; arguments surrounding marriage vows sparked a further interest in God's idea relating to holy matrimony. I heard opinions and witnessed attitudes, which provoked me to chase Scriptural truths. I observed men, treat their wives in church, as well as in the world, disrespectfully. I often wondered why men graced with

Greek text. The word may be displayed in italics, or in parentheses or other brackets, to indicate that it is not in the original text" (Blue Letter Bible).

We understand the insertion is for better readability. However, the exact definition in this particular verse is a military term used for commanding officers over subordinates. We recognize a military commanding officer is responsible for dictating movement over those under authority. The officer commands subordinates to go wherever ordered. They move about according to what they dictate. In a nonmilitary use, it defines a voluntary attitude of cooperating.

"This word was a Greek military term meaning 'to arrange [troop divisions] in a military fashion under the command of a leader." In nonmilitary use, it was "a voluntary attitude of giving in, cooperating, assuming responsibility, and carrying a burden" (Blue Letter Bible).

The words in verses 21 and 24 in Ephesians *"submitting yourselves'* and *'is subject'* have like meaning. In verse 21, "submit" references, Christ Church, and describes proper relations between believers. Scripture teaches Christ's community of believers interacts with love, affection and adoration for each other; preferring the other above self, with a sweet response. The relation within the church's community establishes itself on love.

These associations are not indicative of dictatorial relations. No one presumes control over another; instead, Christ's body responds preferring one to the other in love. Scripture explains a love relation and reverence for Christ. We should esteem one another above self, and yield ourselves in a manner reflected of love. How do we yield? We agree in *love*, and resist divisiveness. Husband and wives ought to respond in like fashion toward each other.

God has fixed an order for everyone in life. I want the reader to understand the context of the word as it applies to the relations of God's people. This same understanding applies to relations between husband, and wife. The relation is one of honor and respect predicated on love, not dictatorship, or military command. It is a voluntary surrender, to an orderly arrangement created by God.

With that said, let me be clear. A wife's agreement with her own husband's leadership is not void. There is a reason Scripture teaches a wife to agree with her *own* husband. It infers her attachment to him and the intimacy between them. She ought not yield, or comply with another man's lead. She is to surrender to her own husband's alone. No one can tell another man's wife what to do. He does not have the responsibility, neither the authority, nor the God-given right to guide the affairs of another man's 'good thing.'

A wife ought to comply with her husband's leadership not dictatorship. I say not dictatorship because God never directed a husband to force his wife's compliance. If he is trying to compel compliance, he must step back and take a close look at himself. God created a woman to yield to the tangible expression of love. If his wife does not have the will to yield, he should inventory himself to find, 'what he lacks in his demonstration of love.'

A husband, who wants to represent himself as the leader in his home, guides by the love he illustrates. In contrast, a husband driven by his egocentric ideologies, may indeed love his family, but is often insensitive by his inflated superiority. When a husband's leadership can govern by unconditional love, his household will build into a loving and thriving society within his home. If he leads by his ego, he is usually coarse and indifferent, as his ideologies prescribe his rigid guidance. Without expressed love, the society within his home is typically in turmoil and struggling in dysfunctional relations.

How does Christ lead us? He leads by aiming us toward every good in life. He openly expressed His love for us on the world's stage, and His expression of love continues to penetrate our hearts today. He taught with love and kindness, so we turn to Him to surrender our love, because of the impact his love has made on us. He is our life coach, always leading us into what is favorable. A husband's disposition ought to be so toward his wife.

Military ideas do not express loving relations between husband and wife. The husband is a leader, not commanding officer. How does a husband effectively lead? He leads by love. The marital union breathes and lives through the rule of love. Love is gentle, and love is kind. The husband displays such passion first, and the wife yields to the love expressed. As J. Vernon McGee so eloquently states,

> *"Woman is the responder, and man is the aggressor: the man is to say, "I love you," and he is the one who does the proposing. She is the one to say, "Yes." No woman is asked to say, "I love you" to a man until he says, "I love you." When a man says he has a cold wife, it is because she has a cold husband. He is not being the husband he should be. It is not her business to be the aggressor. Her role is the sweet submission of love."*

Christ said, 'If you love Me, you will obey my commandments. You will follow where I lead, and hear my Words." Christ's affection for the church is personal and intimate. The affections between husband and wife should reflect that intimacy. A wife responds to the love her husband displays and what she hears broadcast through his words.

Walking in Unity

The wife occupies a position of equality with her husband. They are equal in the eyes of God. The husband is not superior to his wife, or the wife inferior to her husband. Their roles are equally important as well as different. God arranged their positions; He chose one to lead, and one to agree with leadership. God appointed the husband with the responsibility to lead his family, and chose not to charge the wife with such concerns. God appointed her the responsibility to agree with his leadership.

We ought not misunderstand, and think a woman is inept. A woman can lead. We have evidence, of her competence within various professions in our society. However, regarding leadership in the home, God did not charge this duty to her. He chose the husband to handle and fulfill the responsibility.

Let us understand; the husband does not solely determine his leadership alone. His wife acts as his consultant. Her wisdom is his asset. In his decision-making process, she helps frame the utmost result. It is thoughtless, and negligent to dismiss conferring with her mind on any subject matter. God fashioned woman to be the help of man. In the relation of husband and wife, she is his closest confidant, earnest supporter, and his greatest ally.

God positioned the husband as the head of the community within his family. Within this supernatural union, Scripture says, 'the wife is as the husband's own body.' (Ephesians 5:28) God blends the husband and wife into one human being, to become one flesh. (Ephesians 5:31) God unites the husband to his wife as the head, and joins the wife to her husband as his physical body. Both head and body move in unity to ambulate compatibly.

The head and body must agree. If not, they will pull apart. Head and body must move in unity, harmony, and agreement to advance. Otherwise, it tears itself asunder. What is non-adaptive to work in the order created will eventually break apart. This is essential to your understanding.

The head assumes the greatest responsibilities. Headship must consider the needs of its body, and develop means to supply, and aid those needs. It considers the safety and ponders methods to guard the body against threats and dangers. The husband is the visionary of his home, looking beyond his present situation into his future. He seeks God for himself, and on behalf of his family. He stands in the gap as priest and prophet of his home.

The weight of responsibility laid on the head carries a great burden on the husband. This is one reason Scripture teaches the head to love his body. The husband's responsibility to cover, protect, and provide can be a consuming challenge. It is important that he demonstrate his leadership from a position of love, and not his frustration. Without love acting as the barometer, the head can fill with excessive thoughts of provision, and snuff the heart's compassion to fulfill its commitment with love and kindness.

With the body clothed: fed, protected, kept, and cared for. It finds itself nurtured: nourished, covered, defended, and safe. These enrichments nourish health and sustain the body's life. Scripture teaches the body, or wife, to respect and honor her head, which provides its nourishment. If the wife does not remind herself of the respect and honor, her husband deserves, she can become demanding, spoiled and unappreciative; loaded with false expectations; and blinded by what she receives, instead of recognizing what he deserves.

For a cohesive union, head ought to yield to its body, and the body ought to yield to its head. Yielding is agreement between head and body to move together. It is a sweet romantic union, smothered in love, intense intimacy, and deep devotion with the utmost of mutual respect.

Understanding God's Word

God's Word opened my understanding. He enabled me to capture small nuggets of the husband's responsibility as the loving leader, and the wife's responsibility as a willing responder. I began to sense God's way. "I realized His idea needed a raised consciousness in both husband and wife. If each chose God's idea, both would find His thoughts lovely, downright good, sweet, and yummy. His teaching is beautiful."

Well, you need to read the rest of the book and find what I learned. His way, is one full of desire and delight. I promise you God's way is so much sweeter. His indulgence is an ambition to aim for when understood.

Men and husbands, it will enlighten you about God's expectation of you and the responsibility He has placed on your shoulders. It will help you understand what God means when He said, "Love your wife." A challenge perhaps, but one God equipped you to handle.

Love

Agapao is the Hebrew word for love. Agapao means: take delight in the object loved; welcome; entertain; be content at, or with a thing; and to prize above all other. It means the heart's unwillingness to throw or cast away. It also means, be fond of, love dearly and well pleased. A husband should desire his wife's good, and thoughtfully consider her well-being. Show compassion towards her, hold the utmost respect for her, and display it.

God fortified man with everything he needs to become the husband He created. He made him capable to display love and affection toward his wife. "It is beautiful when men understand how they are to love their complement the way God intended." God designed women to want love, and He created man to want honor and respect. Both yearn to satisfy what God placed in them.

Women and wives, I hope you will learn how great and magnificently formed you are by God. You are the window that brings forth life into this world. You are an incredible wonder. I hope this will help you grasp who you are, and why God adorned you with wonderful attributes. I am confident you will understand God's will for your care.

I hope what you read will illuminate your mind. I hope you close this book with a better understanding of the meaning, "submit," regarding both husband and wife. I hope that this work will strengthen, and encourage your heart. I hope you understand, why at times; you react the way you do.

I hope the family, and the children of God will take a fresh look at God's idea for His sons and daughters, and at least consider what He teaches. I hope we agree with God's order and glorify Him in our holy matrimony. When husband and wife align with God's guidance, each can equally receive what the act of submission awards; a wife overtaken by love and a husband receiving honor and respect. It is a romantic dance, which is sweet, spiritual, humanly sensual, and sanctioned by God.

Chapter One

Forgiveness

I have often said, "Forgiveness is not solely for the person who committed an offense. It is equally necessary for the one offended." An offended person believes that if they forgive the offense and offender, it releases them of their guilt. That is what forgiveness does...forgive and release. However, offended hearts resist accepting this truth.

Blinded by the offense, and the resistance to let go; they refuse to commit their heart to forgive. They believe the pain is too grievous an injury to exculpate. Therefore, because of the grave hurt and severe pain, offended people hold their afflictions close. They clinch to the pain as if it were a weapon to ward off any future threats of heartache.

Often, offended people drown in their own hurt and anguish. They refuse to forgive and release the person who affected the wrong, as well as the offense done against them. Through their painful eyes, they have become blind, not seeing the need to release or forgive the guilty. They believe the wrongdoing was too devastating and the pain unjustifiably. The inability to forgive can cause people to relive the act of the offense repeatedly, even if it occurred five, ten, or twenty years prior. The realism of present life smothers in past pain.

Negative pain left untreated affects all manner of life. Untreated pain hinders cultivation of healthy relations. God graced us with this rewarding pleasure, the capacity to spend our lives with other people. Pain infringes upon this desire to spend. We withhold giving, loving, laughing, and living life, as hurt restricts our forward movement to continue to spend or love.

Pain causes us to feel as though we are spent, leaving us too afraid to give anything else. It causes us to feel we already emptied ourselves of all we had. "Enough already, I can take no more, I have nothing left to give, I have had enough." Although alive, people stop living at the point of pain, and life has the tendency to pass by them. In truth, we spend our heart every day, on joys as well as sorrows, sadness as well as gladness.

Pain is exhausting and humiliating, numbing the best of vibrant souls. What value does life offer, if too numb to spend life? The living spends life on hurt and pain, pleasure and gladness. Life comes with a number of surprises, some to our delight, and some to our dismay. Nevertheless, God bestowed life upon us to live, and to live fully, in spite of obstacles. Who wants to live and die unspent, having not given their all? What we learn from life's experiences are priceless.

We are going to spend our lives on many happenings in life; unfortunately, on occasion, it includes a measure of suffering. Our journey through life is part pleasure and part pain. At times, more pain than pleasure. We welcome pleasure while despising pain; after all, why the need to suffer? We prefer to live without the cost of any displeasure. However, when we learn to lean on God, and cast our cares upon Him, He is faithful to strengthen us through every discomfort.

Casting the whole of your care [all your anxieties, all your worries, all your concerns once and for all] on Him, for He cares for you affectionately and cares about you watchfully (1ˢᵗ Peter 5:7AMP).

As long as we are alive, life will present a host of circumstances, which will shape, form, and stretch us beyond our own imaginary limits. We experience good, bad, and the indifferent mixed into the cycle of our life. Painful experiences, though unwanted, heighten our understanding and provoke a compassion for others we would not encompass. A crisis can turn into a powerful testimony to inspire others who endured similar hardships.

Pain is a part of our human experience. It is like an unexpected thief you did not expect. It surprises you. It strikes in places we did not necessarily anticipate, and though we must suffer it, we cannot let the heartache become paralyzing. How do we stop it, and end the pain? One-way to lessen the sting is through forgiveness. Forgiveness not only releases pain, but also releases you from the weight of not forgiving.

God's Grace

God grants us the grace to overcome misfortunes. He placed within our spirit the power to forgive. If we refuse the grace given to us, we embitter ourselves by denying what we can overcome. When we deny God's gift of forgiveness, we hold to pain we can release. Unreleased pain will birth fear. Fear will spread like a wildfire through all areas of life. It impedes the ability to trust. If fear indoctrinates you, you will expel people you should embrace, and judge people by what you have suffered. You will see through fear and pain, which disqualifies the reason to forgive. You will live, just not to the fullest extent possible.

A broken heart does not forgive easily, and brokenness is susceptible to its destruction. People the closest feel the greatest impact. Heartbroken people, who do not forgive, become bitter.

21 Then Peter came and said to Him, "Lord, how often shall my brother sin against me, and I forgive him? " Up to seven times", he asked? 22 Jesus said to him, "I do not say to you, up to seven times, but up to seventy times seven (NASB).

When he finished quoting the Scripture, he asked the congregation, "How many times is seventy times seven?" He answered, "Four-ninety. Four hundred and ninety times a day is how many times you are to forgive someone who offends you. He said, 'I do not think someone offends anyone that many times in one day. If someone offends you, just say 490.'"

The congregation laughed; however, we understood exactly what he meant. I smiled, while saying to myself, "I will keep that sermon on the tip of my mind." When he closed his powerful message, sure enough, before service ended, I had to apply the 490 principle.

While on my knees praying for someone, another person passed me while kneeing me in the head. Imagine that! I received a single blow to my head while petitioning God. Now let me ask, "Do you think you could retain the spiritual tenacity to continue your petition?" I tell you of a truth. The force stopped my prayer for about fifteen seconds, but who is counting.

Within those fifteen seconds, "I thought what was so important for the hurry." I recognized the person's voice as they rushed past me. While still on my knees with my eyes closed, I continued petitioning God on the behalf of the person with whom I prayed. I did not want my temporary distraction to undermine the effectiveness of my prayer. I gathered myself and continued to pray. I let it go. So I thought.

You notice the phrase in the last sentence, "I let it go, so I thought." Ok, here comes the truth. Now, when I finished praying, I reflected on what happened and considered addressing the person, since I recognized their voice. I deliberated my approach, and carefully considered what I would say. I could feel an irritation rise.

Now as I considered the reasons for making my injury known, a thought interrupted my calculating mind, "What are you doing?" The thought stopped me in my tracks. I realized the reason for my premeditated actions were not appropriate. Honestly, after God graciously interrupted my prideful notions, I *knew* my actions would not have been fitting.

Pride can mess you up. You see; it was not the fact that I felt a brisk knee smash into the side of my head. It was the individual's nerve to ignore me as though nothing happened. I thought surely, "You must have felt the impact." I realized my feelings suffered the greatest injury, not my head.

It never ceases to amaze me how feelings can prompt you to engage in an otherwise "walk- a- way" predicament, especially after looking at my own. If you are not careful, your pride will cause you to act indignant. Thank God for saving me from my foolishness, a thought, fueled by pride; provoking my disposition. It reminded me of how often we respond to what we feel instead of reacting intellectually to what we know. I too am guilty. However, thank God, through His mercy, we receive grace to act spiritually proper.

The Principle in Marriage

Several years ago I sat in a courtroom for a divorce proceeding. After many years of marriage, a friend decided to divorce her husband. The Judge called her to the stand and asked her reason for separation. She began with a problem, which occurred, many years prior. I listened as she explained what took place. I sat perplexed, as she told stories which occurred at her grandmother's home. Her grandmother had gone to see the Lord some time ago. After a few minutes, I realized the accounts she related occurred more than twenty-five years ago. She recalled several incidents of assault before their marriage.

After the proceedings, I drove home puzzled. We lived-in distant cities, and saw each other on occasion. However, she never expressed any abuse, and always spoke about doing well and enjoying her life.

I reflected on what she said and questioned, "What madness has she lived?" She did not say the physical assaults continued. However, she expressed she suffered mistreatment years ago. Interestingly, her allegations were not contingent upon any current charges. What she made clear was this; what happened twenty-five years ago still grieved her soul. She never forgave, therefore never healed from past hurt.

Twenty-five years later, her heart still needed healing from those early years. Her original injury became the foundation on which all other offenses; hurts; pains; injuries, and bruises grew. Every offense after the initial one built a fortress of bitterness and eventual hatred for her husband. She did not forgive those first accounts and held those charges against him. She did not like him or love him, and she later told me she just could not live with him anymore.

Traditional Ideas

God created marriage as a close and intimate union between husband and wife. Yet, for some it seems a difficult commitment. How do you build a marriage? On what premise do men and women base their ideology? My husband and I are marriage coaches in our ministry. During our coaching sessions, interestingly, both husband and wife share examples of the role of their father or mother. They explain their parents' conduct and believe what they witnessed is the model for their marriage. They grasp similar expectations and even believe in tolerating certain behaviors.

Usually, both parties extract behaviors they think they should mimic. Somehow, each sees their marriage through observations of their parents. They believe it is the foundation for building their own union. They do not understand what perhaps worked in their parents' home will not work in theirs.

These ideas quickly frustrate, as husband and wife do not understand their futile methods. A husband ought to understand his wife is not his mother, nor is he her father. Neither husband nor wife should expect their spouses to resemble their parent in quality or form. These are false hopes, which create dissatisfaction toward either spouse. "Parents may be the first example, but not all examples are necessarily the best for your unique union."

Married couples must live in the reality of their own marriage. They must discover the healthiest and most productive way for them to live, based on understanding each other. Through understanding, they must learn how to build a great and thriving marriage. When trying to incorporate someone else's ideas into their marriage, it causes conflict. The expectations are false. A husband and wife must figure out between themselves what works best for their marriage.

We encourage married couples to see themselves as, "The Team." We encourage them to understand the responsibility they choose to impose on the other. The team decides and agrees on roles and responsibilities, according to what works best in their unique marriage. The team decides how well they work and flow with one another. They can choose to blend effortlessly, or choose a hellish struggle. Husband and wife must decide the union they want to build. In addition, reminding themselves to support one another as they build.

Do you remember when you first met your heartthrob? The excitement you experienced in the presence of your love. The respect and honor you held for them. The joy you felt when asked to help and the pleasure associated with satisfying their need. These characteristics cannot dissipate. You learn how to continue in respect and honor, love and adoration.

Whatever you did to capture the heart, whatever kindness, whatever gentleness, whatever passion, whatever manner of love yielded, must be upheld, and by no means allowed to lessen. The

mutual compassion one human can contain for another. Marriage is two souls occupying one heart. God created marriage as the deepest form of companionship. Marriage is a spiritual union in natural form. A divine relation created of God. Therefore, He hates dismemberment of marriage.

> *God, not you, made marriage. His Spirit occupies even the smallest details of marriage. And what does he want from marriage? He wants children of God; that's what! So guard the spirit of marriage within you. Don't cheat on your spouse.*

> *I hate divorce," says the God of Israel. God-of-the-Angel-Armies says, "I hate the violent dismembering of the 'one flesh' of marriage." So watch yourselves. Don't let your guard down. Don't cheat* (Malachi 2:15-16) The Message Bible.

When Jesus walked among the Pharisees, there were two opposing schools of thought. One thought held by the school of Hillel, contended that a man might divorce his wife for various causes. However, his reasons unconnected to any infringement of the marriage vow. He could divorce simply because he had ceased to love his wife, or had seen someone whom he liked better. He could divorce his wife just because she cooked his dinner badly. The school of thought held by Schammai taught strict doctrine, but allowed divorce. Schammai permitted divorce only in cases of fornication, adultery, or some offenses against chastity (*The Pulpit Commentaries*).

When the Pharisees came to Jesus Christ, they asked:

> *"Is it lawful for a man to divorce his wife for any reason?" He answered them, "Haven't you read that the one who made them at the beginning 'made them male and female' and said, 'That is why a man will leave his father and mother and be united with his wife, and the two will become one flesh'? So they are no longer two, but one flesh. Therefore, what God*

has joined together, man must never separate." They asked him, "Why, then, did Moses order us 'to give a certificate of divorce and divorce her'?" He said to them, "It was because of your hardness of heart that Moses allowed you to divorce your wives. But from the beginning, it was not this way. I tell you that whoever divorces his wife, except for sexual immorality, and marries another woman commits adultery" (Matthew 19:3-9 International Standard Version).

Moses allowed men to give their wives a letter of divorce, because of hardness, perverseness, and obstinacy of their hearts toward their wives. A husband in those days did whatever he wanted to rid himself of his wife. Moses permitted husbands to give their wives a letter of divorce, mainly to prevent further vicious cruelty. Men of that day were habitually evil, and openly displayed ill-treatment and contempt toward their wives. Men were so horrible and malicious they would go as far as murdering their wives to get rid of them. Does this not still have a familiar ring?

The letter of divorce allowed by Moses granted permission to allow men to free their wives instead of treating them inhumanly. The letter showed an assigned time through procedures with duties to obviate the effects of sudden passions or impulses. The procedure was necessary for thought and reflection. The divorce became public. It compelled publicity, in an effort not to take divorce rashly or lightly. There was a clause of specific language included in the letter, which read, "You are free to marry any man." The clause protected the x-wife from any allegation of infidelity, should she want to remarry.

What Jesus Christ explained was and is, the original foundation of holy matrimony implemented by God, beginning with Adam and Eve. God intended to mirror the beginning relation throughout all the ages. Christ confirms God's original declaration and reinstates the first order of marriage in Matthew 19:3-9.

Both men and women throughout time petitioned for countless divorces. Thank God, His grace forgives. Forgiveness is for both parties, because no one wins in divorce. Divorce shatters everyone involved, not only the husband and wife, but children as well. All people involved must try to recuperate from a divorce's destruction. The gravity of pain suffered is a distress only God can heal for each person. In fact, He is willing and desirous to heal, more than the afflicted heart yearns healing.

We act in such contrary ways. A mess we are; but "God's grace is greater than our mess, and His forgiveness more plentiful than our guilt." His love overpowers any shame in which we might condemn ourselves. He is generous in His love and will heal and restore us.

Marriages face challenges, some more difficult than others, and they can leave scars. A spouse can afflict hurt unintentionally, as well as, intentional. We know people act in malignant ways. Whether unintentional, unthinkable, or just destructive, we must forgive to move forward. Let go and live.

> *When you're hurting so bad,*
> *And you don't know what to do.*
> *You can't let go,*
> *Of the one who's injured you.*
> *Your mind is troubled,*
> *From the thoughts that run within,*
> *You just can't seem to let it go.*
> *You must walk away,*
> *Walk away,*
> *Forgive them and walk away,*
> *Walk away,*
> *490 them and walk away.*
>
> *When you're life's all broken,*
> *You've done all you can do*
> *You've tried and tried,*
> *It's been a challenge for you.*
> *Your heart still aches,*
> *Although you hoped for what was good.*

People don't do what they should.
So you must walk away,
Walk away,
Forgive them and walk away,
Walk away,
490 them and walk away

Forgiveness is for the health of your soul.
It keeps the heart pure and whole.
Frees the mind from the torment within,
Uplifts your soul to rise and live again.
So you walk away,
490 them and walk away,
Forgive them and walk away,
490 them and walk away.
Free you and walk away.
Release them and walk away

~Shadoew

Final Thoughts

Communication is an asset. Not every marriage possesses this attribute. However, it is a necessary tool to achieve clear understanding between spouses. Every married couple should desire to learn the dynamics of communication. It is essential to a healthy marriage. Communicating your thoughts and feelings are crucial in resolving a matter, and dissolving that matter quickly. Do not put it off, and do not spend days walking through your home with unresolved issues. Talk, communicate, and dialogue respectfully. Marriage is teamwork. Husband and wife must agree to walk in harmony. *Can two walk together unless they agree?* Amos 3:3 (King James Version). There should be agreement in directing your marriage.

Please understand, I do not advocate engaging in whatever a spouse wants. I am suggesting agreement in what is healthy, good, and what promotes unity in your holy marriage. I am referring to communicating to understand the heart of the person you married. What do you want to do together? What future do you want to work toward as a couple?

We as human beings strive for individual goals and need the support of our spouse. I am not referring to individual endeavors. As a couple, what do you hope to achieve within your union? What do you hope for in your marriage? Become the team you both want to grow into as partners, friends, lovers, and husband and wife.

Learn grace, and forgive each other. Allow yourselves room to grow. Marriage is a learning experience, and sometimes mistakes happen while you are making memories. You must ask does the good outweigh the bad. Learn each other, and make a conscious effort to apply what you learn. Let understanding resonate and extract what is profitable. If a reason for forgiveness arises, forgive, and after you have, do not recite old accounts or charges of the past. "Be careful and deliberate to forget to remember. However, remember you have forgiven."

Let forgiveness be a good and close friend. Think of it is a set of invisible keys that will unlock doors to heal bitterness: hatred; madness; resentment and anger. Consider the 490 principle and use it wisely. Remember God granted His grace, which enables you to forgive and release. Live in the liberty He ordained for your life. Do not condemn your future by continuing to hold fast to past heartaches. Learn to forgive, and always remember, "Why you fell in love."

Chapter Two

Deception

*W*e can mislead ourselves into situations, which prove hurtful and harmful. In conclusion, we find what we believed, not true. When truth challenges what we thought was true, we become disillusioned and confused about what to believe. Many of us, when we have hoped or believed in something, and it did not occur, it left us shaken, withholding ourselves to further hope again.

How can life exist to the fullest, without the passion to hope for all God has graced us to enjoy? "Hope fuels our inspiration to perform great feats, even when some feats are failures. Nevertheless, we must still pursue hope; it is our stimulus to dream." We learn from unsuccessfulness, and revive ourselves to hope in the truth of what we have learned. We pursue hope relentlessly, never allowing what failed, to be an ally or foundation to abandon our life's expectations. We hope against all odds.

Hope is a great and inspiring desire. It looks beyond present conditions, to believe for more than what presently exists. Hope soars on faith and believes against obstacles. It summons power to change circumstances and surroundings. Without hope, or the deferral of hope, Scripture teaches, 'the heart is made sick or ill.' "Hopelessness is sickness to the soul of man."

Delayed hope makes one sick at heart, but a fulfilled longing is a tree of life. (Proverbs 13:12-GW).

When we deceive ourselves to believe what is not true. God stands with His arms open wide to receive and mend the broken pieces of our shattered lives. We can run to Him for complete recovery. Only God can heal and restore a soul to complete wholeness again.

False Belief

In my late teens, early twenties, I had the privilege of knowing a beautiful young woman. She was outgoing, funny, filled with life and full of adventure. We spent most of our time laughing until our stomachs ached, about nothing of any real importance or consequence. We had no genuine problems in our lives. She was slightly taller than I was, with long blonde hair, a Barbie doll face, and curvaceous frame. We thought we were oh so cute, with our small little waistlines and trimmed silhouettes. How fun being young.

With a lack of motivation to style her hair, she wore it straight, banged, and over her forehead. Summer had arrived and the heat from the sun kissed the valley floor and called for short shorts and tank tops. Although the weather was scorching, life under the clear blue sky was enjoyable. It was a new season and a perfect time for a fresh hairdo. Of course, since I enjoyed styling hair, I suggested pinning those straight flat strands into flowing golden locks. We were so excited.

I pinned curled her hair and sat her under the dryer. For about an hour, we eagerly awaited hoping for supermodel results. Finally, the time came to remove the pins. We were so nervous; we did not know what to expect. I removed one pin. Oh my, a shiny cylindrical curl fell past her shoulder. Gorgeous locks of curls from the first hairpin to the last. Every single curl was perfect. Her hair was stunning; shining like the sun, and full of bounce, and flowing with curls.

The results amazed us both. Her hair turned out better than we expected. Of course, I came up with the idea. Those golden locks were just *"gorgiful"* (That is gorgeous and beautiful combined. When you are young, you make up words not in the dictionary). Her flat and lifeless hair transformed into bounce, body, and shine. She was so thrilled and eager to go home and show off her new hairdo to her "Bo." Equally excited, I knew he would love her beautiful head of hair as well.

The following day, I heard a knock on the door. When I opened the door, she stood there banged and straight again. I immediately asked, "What have you done? What did you do to your hair?" She said, "I washed it out." "Why did you wash the curls out of your hair? It looked so good." She looked me in my eyes and said, "He did not like it, and he made me wash it out!"

We stood staring at each other. While standing in the middle of the floor, her eyes glassed over, and tears formed in the bottom of her lids. I said, "Why didn't he like it?" "He didn't like it" she said. "He didn't like my hair!" She was crying hysterically, so I made her sit down on the couch to try to calm her down. She said, "He grabbed me by my hair, and dragged me around on my knees. I stared at her motionless. For a moment I could not think, I could not talk.

We sat and stared at each other for what seemed like eternity. Out of the silence, she said, "He drugged me by my hair and pulled my hair out of my head." She bent over and began pulling up her pant legs. When the hem of her pant crested over-the-top of her left knee, anxiety struck. I sighed with relief, a few scrapes, and scratches. As she lifted her pant leg over her right knee, an open red wound appeared. A portion of the skin on her knee was gone, anxiety struck again.

How surreal, slowly I began thinking, "Why, just because she decided to comb her hair?" I had never seen her boyfriend act like this before. Witnessing the effects of his behavior was shocking. I could not believe he did not love her hair. It was so beautiful.

Alarmed, I became afraid for her safety. A man ought never to raise his hand against a woman under any circumstance. My circle of family and friends taught: Men who behave in such a manner are cowards. They beat on women, but they would not fight another man. These kinds of men choose to overpower someone who is weaker, and not as strong or stronger. They resist raising their hand against someone who will challenge them. So, to hear her describe how he dragged her around by her hair, did not sit well with me at all.

We talked for quite some time. I tried to encourage her to leave, but she said, "He was sorry for what he had done, and he won't do it again." "How do you know he won't, how do you know?" I said. "Because I know he loves me, and I love him," she replied. Her words troubled me more than his assault. I knew she believed what he told her. She persuaded me that she believed in what he said. She spoke about his love with such confidence.

Evil

When ten years old, I saw a man repulsively beat a woman on the street. Interestingly, I could not recall seeing her before the day of the crime, although she lived one door down from my family. I witnessed her exhaust herself trying to defend her life. Her attempts proved useless as fists and kicks repeatedly struck her body.

Watching a man assault, a pregnant woman was hideous and evil. It was one of the worst evils I ever witnessed one human inflict on another. The images I vividly recalled were her failed attempts to protect her unborn child. Her pregnancy was obvious. Yet, he violently kicked her in the stomach. He would draw his foot back and thrust it into her abdomen repeatedly.

People were standing around watching, while others tried to stop him. I remember how horrible and sorrowful I felt for her. No one could help her escape the vicious beating. Sadly, the one who caused the torment happened to be the one with whom she shared her home, her husband. I recall thinking, "How does she run away." "Where can she run and hide from someone like him?" "She should disappear?" In one moment as a child, I knew I could never endure such grievous contempt.

As she spoke about his love for her, this hideous incident flashed through my mind. I instantaneously found myself standing on the sidewalk again. I could hear her vaguely, in the distance. Her voice drew me back to the present as she continued talking. "He loves me. He loves me," I heard her say. I repositioned myself as I regained my divided attention. I told her, "People don't beat people they love. Love does not drag you on your knees by the roots of your hair across the carpet."

Hours passed like minutes, time stopped; as I tried to convince her of the danger she faced by staying with him. I could not change her mind or convince her to leave, or get help. She chose no other alternative. She left for home, and I sat wondering what was to become of her.

A couple of weeks passed, and the doorbell rang. I opened the door. It was a pleasant surprise to see her face smiling. She and I laughed and talked as always. She seemed herself. We laughed like always until our stomached ached. I was so happy I had my friend back. I missed her during those couple of weeks.

We giggled and laughed about nothing. We were just happy to see each other. We kept giggling, laughing, and saying silly things, until she slipped a set of striking words into our laughter. "I have knots in my head." My laughter stopped as I caught her statement through the noise of our silliness. We looked at each other, speechless.

Finally, after several seconds passed she repeated, "I have knots in my head." She asked me to feel them. I felt several lumps on and around the top of her head. I asked her, "Why don't you leave him?" She said, "It's going to get better; he wasn't always like this. I love him, and I know things are going to change. I know he loves me." "If you don't leave him, he is going to keep hurting you. Do you want him to beat you to death? If he has hit you once, he will hit you twice, then three times. He will hit you repeatedly, because he believes he can. A man should never raise his hand against a woman. Do you want him to kill you?" She assured me her difficulty would get better, and he would change, because they love each other.

My disposition towards her boyfriend and her willingness to tolerate his abuse made her uncomfortable. I kept pressing her about why she stayed with him. In her big heart, she believed and convinced herself, he would change, and eventually they would live this wonderful life.

For her sake, I hoped it would come true. She loved him, and willingly gambled her life for what she thought could be possible. She had persuaded herself he would change one day, and her conviction gave her reason to tolerate his abuse until his transformation. She was consistent, and she did not waver in her decision.

Over the last several months when I saw her, the smile I had come to know, stretched less. The loud and giddy laugh I loved so much became a slight chuckle. I could not help but to ask, "Why won't you leave?" She would kindly say, "Things will get better. I love him, and I know he loves me." Her visits soon became less and less frequent until I never saw her again.

Physical and Word Abusiveness

The effects of verbal abuse are devastating. Oral abuse is often more traumatizing than physical abuse. The effects last a lifetime, and can cause psychological disfigurement. Word abuse attacks the mind; and circles within the thought process repeatedly destroying ones image of self.

Verbal abuse can disqualify a person's healthy thought about self. Corrupt words need removal from ones thinking. Often, the affected person needs someone alongside them to speak life and truth. Negative and unhealthy thoughts need a push out the mind. God's thoughts communicated to a person can overturn and cast out negative ideas. Understanding what God said, restores faith in self, and helps a person capture the truth of their person.

Verbal abuse is treacherous because it attacks the thoughts of a person, and chips away at one's belief about self, and blinds a person's image of his or her own worth. It attacks the foundation of a person's faith, sabotages hope, and undermines belief. It robs a person of true worth. It leaves them empty, sometimes hard as a rock, and sometimes fragile as an eggshell. Word abuse breaks down the healthy thoughts, and strips the conscious of every good opinion about self.

Our opinions we entertain about self-need to be healthy. Scripture teaches whatever we think about ourselves so we are. If we think we are nothing, we act like nothing. When we think we are something, we act like something. If we believe ourselves to do anything, we will strive to reach those objectives. If we believe ourselves to do nothing, we take on little, and witness no real growth in our lives. How we think and consider ourselves controls if we live in greatness or not.

"For as he thinks within himself, so he is"
(Proverbs 23:7 NASB).

Words are Powerful

When we were children, there was a nursery rhyme, "Stick and stones may break my bones, but words will never hurt me." What a lie we chimed to those who injured and affected our psychological and emotional security. We have learned how words can build or tear down the human soul.

Words have the ability to frame greatness, or kill the dream in a human soul. If "life words" enter the ears of someone continually, they live, grow, and thrive. When someone speaks words of death in someone's ears, overtime, faith in self darkens. They stumble through the voices of negative words. Their dreams suffocate underneath the voice of deathly influence. Their life exists under the power of word curses stemmed from declarations of untruths. God created every person with purpose and vision for his or her life.

People who curse the minds of other people with words are "dream killers." The negative effects stunt a person's ability to think beyond what they heard. They become stagnate in faith, and in the pursuit of their dreams.

Word Curses

Years ago, I remember a girlfriend who always dressed like a Saks Fifth Avenue woman. Her hair styled with makeup perfectly applied. When she married, her husband began telling her she was stupid, ugly, and that she did not have any sense. Eventually, she stopped styling her hair, avoided wearing makeup, and discontinued managing her well-manicured appearance.

She and I would converse about the words he spoke to her. She would express what he said and how he said it. I would reply by saying, "You are not stupid, you are intelligent. You are not ugly; you are beautiful. He told her he no longer wanted me to come to their home. I honored her husband's request. Somehow, his words penetrated her mind, and she began to believe what she heard. Everything about her changed; her physical appearance as well as her spirit.

Subsequently, he threw her out of a moving vehicle. She lived through the accident with not only scares from the placement of pins in her ankles, but the ones carved across her heart. I saw her years after, still as beautiful, but not as vibrant, a slight limp in her gait.

People spend years trying to hurdle over damaging words. Some people recover quicker than others do. Words are powerful. God created all that exists with His spoken Word. Whether words are spoken positively or negatively they shape and frame thoughts in the mind.

Physical abuse may heal, but the nightmare effects, which occurred during the abuse, lock into memory. These memories can become psychologically challenging. Verbal abuse as well as, physical abuse both requires time and often counseling to recover and heal.

Who Can Change?

Countless women believe their love is enough to cause change in the one they want. They convince themselves their love will convert his abusive behavior into conduct they desire. Many women have born witness to these failed beliefs. Even though they loved, their love was not enough. Some survive to tell of it, while the speechless tell their stories through someone else.

Love can provoke the heart to change! However, the desire to correct a flawed disposition must deliberately come from within the flawed individual. Love will not change any man, or woman for that matter. A man or woman must choose to change and submit their heart to love. If neither chooses to humble themselves, change will not occur; "change is a choice."

God through Jesus Christ can change the condition of a man's heart. Christ transforms a man's heart beyond anything he commits to doing by himself. If he allows God to heal and correct him, he can become a beautiful human being. One who can love God; love and cherishes his woman; and learn how to glue to his wife. Women ought to consider this statement as well.

Love seeks reciprocity, and sometimes love finds love, and sometimes not. Interestingly, when not, some believe, 'if I love him enough, he will love me in return.' How untrue. Besides, a woman should never precede a man's affections. A man ought to surrender his heart before she ever yields hers. God created a woman to respond to love. He did not create her to love hard enough to cause a reciprocal response. She is the weaker vessel. God created woman to respond to loves' strength, and loves' cover.

No one can make a person love; neither can love *force* one to love either." Individual hearts choose whom they want to love, and who not. Love is a decision of conscious commitment. "The heart of every man decides on whom he wants to spend his love." It is the natural order of God for a man to find, not for a woman to be searching for...

People believe love is a passion or feeling. Love is a passion you can feel. As you well know, passions and feelings come and go. People love today, trip and fall in love with someone else tomorrow; it is that easy. Why does this happen? People live in a host of emotions. Feelings now are preconditions, instead of commitment the standard.

When feeling dissipate so does the so-called love. Love commits to the object of its affection. "Passions, feelings and love mean nothing if not dedicated, committed, and attached to the individual loved." Love defines more than just feelings. Love is an eternal commitment to another person. Committed love seals two hearts, and glues them together. Scripture teaches:

> *"Love is patient, love is kind. It does not envy; it does not boast; it is not proud. It is not rude; it is not self-seeking; it is not easily angered, and it keeps no record of wrongs. Love does not delight in evil but rejoices with the truth. It always protects, always trusts, always hopes, and always perseveres". (1st Cor 13:4-7 New International Version).*

No Abuse by God's Standard for Women

God did not create the woman in her magnificent form to suffer the abuses of men. He formed her to receive loving-kindness, nurture, care, honor, and respect. She needs understanding from her husband, or her "Bo". He should apply his mind to understand her intrigue, as well as, recognize her as being weaker than he is.

A man ought to show and exercise acts of kindness toward her, because of her lack of strength. She is 'by no means considered to be lower in intellect, but in physical strength only.' He should recognize she tires more easily than he does, and he should properly consider her fragility.

How many men allow God to teach them the truth about Scriptural marital relations? Teaching not handed down from cultures, or interpretation, rather teaching by God's Word. The truth about how God instructs a husband to behave toward his own wife, and if unmarried toward his woman.

A wealth of knowledge lay throughout the pages of Scripture should one want to educate his mind in Godly principles. Many men are ignorant of God's teaching as well as women. How many choose to discount His instruction to interpret according to passed down teachings?

Does it not say God made them male and female in His image, and blessed them to both subdue and conquer? Why a disparity, are husband and wife both not heirs to God's Kingdom? Opposing attitudes and behaviors toward women are against God's teaching. All God's daughters deserve care according to God's idea.

God gifted women to husbands to love, cherish and protect. God's mind toward His daughters is good, and He does not abuse whom He loves. He covers and protects, loves and cherishes, provides and sustains. He cares deeply for His loved ones, so ought a man for his woman, and his wife.

"God blessed them, and God said to them, "Be fruitful, multiply, fill the earth, and subdue it. Rule the fish of the sea, the birds of the sky, and every creature that crawls on the earth" (Genesis 1:28 HCSB).

"Husbands, go all out in your love for your wives, exactly as Christ did for the church--a love marked by giving, not getting" (Ephesians 5:25 The Message Bible).

Daughters, learn God's expectation for you. As a woman, He created you to nurture and for nurturing. He built you to experience deep affection, and know love's protection. Measure men by God's standards not the worlds, and desire care the way God intended.

All women want to experience love, and give love; God fashioned woman this way. Nevertheless, a woman ought not to run seeking to fulfill her own thirst. How many found, after running, they ran into madness? Madness, which resulted in picking up splintered pieces of their heart, and the necessity to remove unwanted residue from their life.

God's grace is sufficient to heal anything. "If you feel splintered or shattered, God's grace is overwhelming. Ask God, He will help you put the pieces together. No matter what your heart endured, God is a restorer of the brokenhearted. Nothing is impossible for God to heal and restore. He will make you laugh again and restore confidence in you; while learning how to love and express love." He created you to experience love and all its beauty. Understand God's expectation of passionate love for you.

Chapter Three

Silent Sufferer

ou can never tell what a person has experienced, especially, when they learned how to smile and cover their hardship. Some people suffer and you see it written on their face. Other people cloak and hide their trouble, appearing to have no misfortune as they mask what they bear. I call them silent sufferers.

Silent, because they do not tell, no one hears their cry. In silence, they scream, and in quiet, they cry. You cannot detect their trouble. They display no signs of turmoil. They stroll through life appearing normal and happy; smiling under the mask of unbearable pain.

When I began learning, or should I say when women opened their heart, dug inside and pulled out what they had shut away. I learned as they taught. In the beginning, their experiences saddened me. I looked at some as weak and easy. How very wrong

I was. I soon realized through their perseverance and forbearing spirit they possessed enormous resilience and inner strength. Strength, which left me in awe of them.

In my late twenties, I met an incredible woman. She was bright, and articulate with a great sense of humor. Our first conversation captivated my interest as she spoke of her life. She grabbed my curiosity. She intrigued me. Her stories carried me through her past and brought me back into the current day. I listened carefully to each of her accounts and found myself lost in the wisdom of her words. Her intellect was most attractive.

I enjoyed listening to her wisdom, and soon mustered up enough nerve to ask questions. To my pleasant surprise, she did not hesitate to answer, and even seemed glad I had asked. The perseverance and endurance I heard in her speech fascinated me. Her disposition and demeanor moved me. It was evident she was a woman of enormous resilience and strength. Yet, I detected a hint of delicacy in her voice. She answered with purity, and surprised me by her honesty. I found her delightfully refreshing. She arrested my attention.

On one day in particular, as I visited, I sensed something different about her. She appeared preoccupied, and neither of us said much. She appeared troublesome, and confined to her own thoughts. Patiently, I sat looking through a magazine until I heard her take a deep breath. When she let out a sigh, I raised my head to look at her, and she caught my eyes.

She slightly dropped her head to the left and began to speak. The texture of her voice was soft and low. Something altered. I sensed sorrow. As she began to speak, the tone of her voice forewarned me she was taking me to a dark place. I could hear it in her pitch. A place previously not ventured. It made me a little nervous. I did not know what to expect.

As she spoke, her words drew scenes, like in a picture show. She opened the door to her past, and escorted me through the entrance. My toes curled in my shoes. Her words formed graphic scenes of a former time. Her memory appeared flawless, as her words stroked images across the canvas of my mind. I could see. Carefully, her words drew one incident, after another.

She removed each, as if to lift pieces of layered clothing, leaving nothing except nakedness. She trusted me with her words, and I found her confidence in my ability to hear what she needed to say moving. It was as though, she thought finally, "I have an ear to hear what I have kept silent, and a heart to share my hidden agony."

She spoke of her husband and the years of physical and verbal abuse. She spoke of a time when married, and the reproach she suffered at the hands of her husband. She elaborated on his verbal assaults as well as sharing her physical abuse. Obviously, she still suffered from memories lodged in her mind; memories, which produced evident hurt and pain on this particular day. I listened with overwhelming compassion, and I thought, "Wow, alone with no one to call, yet, look at how strong she is, and what she has survived."

Times of Old

I understood the conditions women tolerated before my generation, and unfortunately witnessed some of its affects. Women did not disclose the negative circumstances within their household. A woman hid her family affairs, unless something pleasurable happened. However, anything not enjoyable she sealed her lips shut. At that point, it became no one's business. Besides, years ago, an unsettling home, rested on the shoulders of the wife. It must be her fault for not keeping a happy home. What has she done?

Women did not want the stigma of failure, or the embarrassment attached to it. Although not at fault, the wife usually received the blame for any unrest in the home. She did not open her mouth to anyone to save face. By doing so, she escaped humiliation, and blame for not creating a harmonious environment. Therefore, women projected an appearance contrary to the truth they lived. Because of their silence, many women suffered secret abuse at the hands of their husbands.

Interestingly, men were the breadwinners in the home; women were unemployed and solely dependent on their husbands, in most cases. For some married, as well as unmarried women, their dependency promoted crises. The husband or supporter understood her dependency on him and her lack of self-support. In some instances, her need proved disadvantageous for her. Without financial support, she found herself mistreated, after all, where could she go without means to care for herself. I remember this one old saying as a young woman, "Keep 'em barefoot and pregnant."

Men behaved badly, if they chose. However, they also expected women to tolerate their misconduct. Men could hang out with the boys, run rancid with other women, and even bring illegitimate children to his home and expect his wife to nurture his illicit offspring. What could she do? She had no place to go and no means to sustain herself. If she did leave, her husband would search for her, and if found, return her to conditions worst than she previously endured. Instead of him caring for, and protecting her; her predicament caused a regretful dependency.

I continued to listen as I sat across from her, and imagined what she endured. Her pain appeared fresh and not far removed from the many years before. It was still alive. She paused, and then said, "I don't know, which is worst, someone saying hard words, or someone laying their hands on you. Either way it hurts. No one knows the suffering I endured. I lived afraid to go to sleep at night, not knowing if I would live until the morning."

She said, "I lived in fear for so long in my own house, not knowing what would happen to me from day to day. My husband was mean. He called me a whore, a tramp, and he accused me of sleeping with other men. He even told me he would bring other men in our house for me. I swear to God; I did nothing wrong, and it hurt me so bad. I have cried many days and many nights. I have cried myself to sleep, after being humiliated, disrespected, and cursed. My husband told me he did not want me, and he said, 'nobody else would want me either.'"

Breaking the Soul

She said, "I was beaten, had my lip busted, my eyes blacked. The same things happen to me over and over again. He pulled my hair out from my head in gobs; I held clumps in my hand. I wondered why he treated me so bad. I asked myself, 'What was wrong with him? How did he get that stuff in his head? Why did he believe all those lies about me? God is my witness. Everything he said about me was a lie.'"

"He made jokes about my body, and I felt so disgraced. My heart bitterly broke, it dried up, and the love I felt he beat it out of my soul, until I could no longer feel anything for him anymore. I looked for love, but I could not find it. Words hurt and kill love in the heart. I went through this for a long time, nobody really knows."

I listened to understand, not judge, just understand; she intrigued me. I found her fascinating, and a woman who possessed enormous strength. "Who is this great woman I sat before?" She seemed so strong. I did not see weakness. I could not see weakness. I saw a determination to survive, and a woman to admire.

I gathered the nerve to ask, "So why did you stay? Why did you not run and find refuge elsewhere? Why didn't you leave?" She said, "Where was I going to go? I had children, where was I going to take them? How were we going to live? I had no job, and I had no money. I had no place to go." "So you stayed for your children," I asked. "There was nowhere for me to go," she said.

Dazed and saddened by her forthcoming accounts. I found myself consumed in what she said, and then considered all the alternatives afforded to me in life. I thought about her age, the ideologies, and opportunities of her day. Women were different then. Today women let their voices rise to bring consciousness to abuse. Even so, women still choose to remain in levels of madness today. Varieties of conditions form their decisions. Women choose to stay in abusive relations, to keep their children stable, for financial security, and because of hope in love.

She allowed me to peak in her life, a snapshot beyond my experience. She took me somewhere unfamiliar. Her words filled my heart with compassion for her. I reflected on her despair. How long had she not spoken? It seemed haunting to hold onto pain for so many years.

Sharing her suffering provoked a deeper respect and appreciation. Her belief that I would be quiet, and listen without interruption and ridicule, I appreciated. Somehow, she must have seen willingness in me to hear her sorrow. For what other reason would she have told such a traumatic story, unless she believed I would care to listen. I was grateful she chose me as the one with whom to share her silenced pain.

She bravely suffered for a greater quality of life for her children. However, her suffering not only broke her heart, but also her spirit. I thought, 'if she perhaps had the means, or the finances to support herself and her children, maybe she could have thwarted some of the heartache. Maybe she could have frustrated the attacks against her person. She could have independently cared for her children on her own, and perhaps escaped the bruises left on her soul.'

I soaked my mind in what she said and concluded, when you do not have anything for yourself; "You must accept what someone else gives to you." My spirit stirred as I considered the results of those consequences. Without disclosing my thoughts, she said, "Make sure you have something for you. Be sure you can stand on your own two feet, and take care of yourself before you tie the knot. You be careful who you marry." I considered it sound advice. However, I knew, not all men caused terror in their homes. I knew good men who loved, treasured, and adored their wives. Nonetheless, I wrote a mental note on a wall in my mind.

I could not stop thinking about everything she said, and I relentlessly wondered, "What if he loved her, what if she experienced love the way she should have? I thought, "The joy she would have received from being cherished." How different her life would have been, smothered in goodness, instead of being shattered and broken. Her memories would have been of things desirous to remember, instead of regret. She would treasure the missing love. However, she had no love to miss. She would have known love and compassion. Now she will never know love's kindness or giving. What a robbery of sorts, to be married, have a husband, but never know his love. Wow, that is madness.

Freedom From The Madness

She recited her first accounts of meeting her husband. "He was a different man at the beginning; he was nice," she said. "As the years progressed, he began to change into another human." She said, 'one, she did not recognize.'" She told me, "He didn't talk about anything or anybody in his life. After many years of watching him, I do not believe he knew how to have relationships with people. He did not want the company of anyone." She asked, "How could you be in this big old world and want to be alone?" I did not respond. She did not ask the question seeking an answer. She continued to say, "I didn't understand his ways. I don't think I ever understood him."

"The last time I saw him, He cursed me. When I saw him the next morning, he was dead. I was not sad he passed. It was as if

God took away my burden, and all my suffering. I was relieved. I felt the burden lift. I was free from heartache and free from hard words." She told me, "I didn't have anything left for him. The love, the thrill; he slowly killed it overtime. He took my love away little by little. The way; he talked to me, and the way he treated me, the thrill was gone. He was so mean!"

Many years passed from the time of her husband's death to the day of our conversation. Her scars still hurt. With caution I asked, "Have you forgiven him?" She turned her head to look me in the eye. Her facial expression said, "You have to be kidding; you did not just ask me a stupid question."

Stunned by her facial language, I hesitated shortly, and then continued, "You have to forgive him; you have to forgive him and let him go. The wrongs he did are behind you now. You no longer need to think about it, or relive it. It is your past. Forgive him, release him, and the horrible acts he did against you. You need to be free. Let God heal you. God wants your life whole and happy. He wants your heart healed and your mind at peace. Please forgive him!"

She was willing to forgive all his faults and release him for what he did. I asked her if I could pray for her, and she agreed.

"God you know the depths of her hurt and pain, you know her years of sorrow. You not only can see her broken heart, but you can feel the gravity of her mourning. You know every word struck her soul. You can see every wound that bleeds. Let her heart forgive every wrong; let her mind release every charge. Heal the cuts and bruises of her heart. God sear the harsh words from her memory and refresh her heart and mind. Restore her joy, laughter, and love. Let this be a recollection that no longer robs her spirit of the life you gifted her to enjoy. Heal and make her complete in love again. God restore and make her whole. Glorify Yourself for her cause. To You, God do I make this decree. Thank you for restoring her soul. In Jesus name, Amen."

Who Are You In God?

We can say, "This should not happen in a Christian home." Unfortunately, it does. Verbal and physical abuse occurs in the homes of Christian families around the world. God calls us to peace, peace especially shown in relations between husband and wife. God's unites husband and wife into one person. In God's eyes, they are one human being.

Why do we harm self? This question eludes the finest of minds, and today we are still without sufficient answers. Women ought never to suffer a man's brutal hand. His hands are to work for her need. They are to draw her near to himself. Peace can never exist in a home when a woman is suffering abuse. The heart scars as well as the mind, and both suffer anguish.

Do not keep abuse hidden. You need help, not only for yourself, but for your spouse as well. Tell someone, you do not have to suffer in silence. There are counselors: therapist; family; friends; people and organizations, which are willing to aid you. Today is a new day and a different era. You are not powerless. You are powerful. God created women with tremendous resilience and strength.

God did not create a woman's body to be a punching bag at the hands of men. A man's hands are to hold, caress, defend, and protect his woman, or wife. From the beginning, God formed women as a delicate vessel for care. She needs nurturing, love, romance, and thoughtfulness.

God made woman to walk aside man: to stroll through life with him, not behind him. Nor did God make her to walk in front of him either. I heard a cliché, "Behind every good man is a good woman." I contend this is a faulty statement. I submit, "On the *side* of every good man is a priceless and invaluable woman." God did not create a woman to walk behind her man, but rather, to walk alongside him.

A husband's responsibility is to lead and help guide his wife through life with his arm locked into hers. Most people believe the husband should lead in front, while the wife follows behind. If she is behind him, how can she clearly hear his voice, or grasp his instructions? A position from behind would severely compromise her vantage point. A woman ought never to walk behind; she should always stroll on his side.

When by his side, she can hear, and respond to every instruction with certainty. At his side, he has access to her ear, and she need not second-guess what he has spoken. She can respond to his words with the utmost of confidence, knowing she heard every word he uttered.

Women identify who you are in God. Know and be acquainted with the daughter God created in you. You must know for yourself what God said regarding you, and His expectation for you. Be not dazed by man's interpretation, but rather, by God's concept. Know God's mind; the One that formed you. Understand God's idea regarding everything. He designed woman to receive sweet love, and careful consideration according to His plan. Know the plan.

Did You Know?

A phenomenon is what domestic violence is considered. It reaches across all classes, race, creed, and color of women. It is true that women have made substantial accomplishments toward the fight against abuse. However, abuse remains an epidemic! Thank God, more women are speaking out, but many women do not report crimes against them. Here are a few noteworthy statistics:

- Every nine seconds, a woman is beaten in the United States. (Source: American Institute on Domestic Violence 2001)
- On average, their husbands or boyfriends in the United States murder more than three women a day. (Source: Family Violence Prevention Fund)

- Domestic violence is one of the most chronically underreported crimes. (Source: U.S. Department of Justice, Bureau of Justice Statistics, "Criminal Victimization," 2003.)

- An estimated 1.3 million women are victims of physical assault by an intimate partner each year. (Source: Costs of Intimate Partner Violence Against Women in the United States. 2003. Centers for Disease Control and Prevention, National Centers for Injury Prevention and Control. Atlanta, GA.)

Chapter Four

Influential Immorality

What is your definition of friend? What measures do you take to allow or integrate friendships into your life? How do you choose as well as become chosen? For most of us, our friendships initiate within family circles, in school, or through the workplace. We begin casual conversations and exchange general information of no consequence.

Gradually, if relationships with a family member, schoolmate, or co-worker evolve into a comfortable and trustworthy bond, during bonding, indiscreet conversations become more pronounced. Private matters further disclosed. We let down our guard and exchange intimate information we should never flippantly talk about.

Our families and co-workers hold great influence over our lives. We give them permission to suggest ideas and concepts, which contain possibilities to alter our course, hopefully for the better. However, this is not always true. A family member, schoolmate, or co-worker's conversations have derailed many husbands and wives, men, women, boy and girl.

People engage in conversations and communicate information, which they should never exchange. Some conversations are valuable, and the information discussed can benefit a person's life. Those are what I call healthy conversations. However, I am not referring to healthy words soaked in wisdom. I infer those words used through conversation, which entangle and influence the mind to consider what it should never regard.

Indoctrination

Look at this particular incident between a husband, wife, and the husband's co-worker. Just in case you are wondering, it is a true story. The husband and his co-worker use an office at their workplace. They share responsibilities; and spend most of their time together. Overtime, they become comfortable with each other and work well in their confined quarters, developing a common like, and mutual respect. They converse daily and come to enjoy one another's company, looking forward to working together.

The co-worker believes their relationship has matured to a confidentiality level. Now at ease, the co-worker decides to share a bit of information about his lifestyle. He is rather excited; and begins to tell the husband how he and his wife enjoyed themselves on the prior evening. The husband responds, "It sounds like you and your wife had a good time; good for you man." The co-worker says, "Yeah, it was decent."

The co-worker continues and describes his indulgence in spouse swapping. The husband surprised and embarrassed by the lurid discourse of information, responds in disbelief. "How could you let another man touch your wife like that? That ain't right man that just ain't right. How could you let a man sex it up with your wife? That ain't something you should wan'na tell somebody!"

The co-worker restrains himself from sharing further details about his swapping experiences. He keeps his conversations work related with some small talk about life's general issues. Several weeks pass, and the coworker invites the husband to a dinner party. The husband accepts, and he and his wife attend the social gathering.

At the dinner party, the co-worker and husband step outside for a breath of fresh air. The co-worker asks the husband, "What do you think about my wife?" The husband responds, "I think she is beautiful. You have a beautiful wife." The husband jokingly says, "How did you get her. She must have picked you. As ugly as you are, I know you didn't pick her, she had to choose you." Both laugh, and the co-worker says, "Yeah she did pick me! She is beautiful, isn't she?"

The co-worker asks, "What do you think about her? What do you think about being with my wife?" "Are you crazy?" says the husband. "Why you are pushing the line on me, I already told you I don't get down like that. Why are you asking me something like that anyway man, I don't want to be with your wife. Thanks for the invite, but I'm out." "Man I apologize. You don't have to leave." "Yes, I do. I'll see you later!" The husband finds his wife and they leave the party.

Over the course of the next several weeks, the co-worker insists on sharing his rendezvous with the husband. Although the husband repeats his request to his co-worker to keep his indiscretions to himself, the co-worker does not honor them. Because the husband assumes a growing interest, the co-worker continues his exhortations. The husband weakens to the co-workers vivid expressions.

Slowly, but surely, the husband becomes entangled as he permits images to seep into his mind's eye, and toy with the fantasy of self. What the husband never considered, he now finds amusing, and willing to consider its indulgence. He struggles with the idea, and fights within, as he wars with the onset of illicit desires.

The more he lends his ear and listens to his co-worker; the intrigue overcomes him as his mind floods with teased imagery. His illicit passions inflame, as he begins to crave a stimulated desire. He has convinced himself of something a short time ago; he thought was appalling. Now his mind delights in entertaining the idea of such acts.

By the influence of his co-worker's conversations, the husband who once rejected the idea now wants to join in spouse swapping. He devises a strategy to introduce the idea to his wife. He rehearses how he is going to pitch the idea to receive a positive response. Bingo, he has it, and a plan initiates.

Persuaded by his desire, he contrives a way to convince his wife to lay her body down with another man, while he does the same with another woman. Driven by the influence of vivid fantasies indoctrinated into his mind by his co-worker, he develops a lust, which blinds him of the acts against his own body, as well as his wife's.

He arranges a dinner date and patiently waits for the suitable moment to pitch the idea to his wife. He senses his timing, and opens the subject matter for conversation. Stunned and revolted at his suggestion, she cannot believe he could ask her such a question. However, because of the mental molestation by the illicit conversations of his co-worker, his thoughts infiltrate with fantasies his flesh now aspires to pursue. He troubles his wife's mind continuously with his idea, until she relents and agrees with his request.

Imagine! The influence of another man's words caused the husband to consider destroying his marriage. The husband blinded and driven by his own lust could not distinguish the influence. He could not identify the molestation seeded into his mind. With his mind molested, he sought an opportunity to take part in consensual sex. He hoped his wife would sanction his misconduct with her blessing to participate. He did not weigh the consequences or effects against his marriage. Unfortunately, they both began swapping.

Friends or Enemies

Friends do not always look like an enemy. They do not usually speak as one either. The devil never appears as the devil, but appears as an angel of light. Warning signals do not always emanate from a person's appearance, or trigger the senses to alarm self of the threat of danger. People are creative at cloaking what they do not initially want unmasked. The threat is not the physical person, but rather, the spirit moving in that physical body.

The spirit releases deadly words, which crawl into the mind, and up from the heart through the mouth, easing across lips, to uproot and tamper with another's life and soul. The influence of words will alter your thoughts, imagination, ideas, and opinions, and turn your mind around to look at what you would never consider. Whether someone speaks good or bad words, words are powerful.

We should employ our conscious and consider the influential words of those who encircle us. Whether we acknowledge it, or not, our influence comes from people, we allow into our lives. Our conversations need analyzing while listening, and before speaking. We should never allow destructive words to seed in us, or come out of us. Every word a person seeds into your hearing literally contains the power to persuade you in one way or another. Consider simple conversation that influenced your decisions. We should always have our antennas raised, listening attentively.

Unfortunately, many of us lack developing our divine spiritual awareness. We are not careful to pay attention to another's spirit. We act gullible, and listen to anything. We lack guarding our ears, from words that drop into our soul, mess with our mind, and affect our lives.

We engage in idle conversations just to be sociable. "Isn't the weather beautiful today? How are you doing? Oh, your hair is lovely." These are general non-invasive, non-intrusive conversations. I am not referencing, general, basic, or mundane conversations, but those more specific targeted ones. I am referring to those conversations that can alter the course of one's life in negative ways.

If negativity continues to filter through a person's hearing, the listener will eventually battle with those negative words. Such relations need reevaluating. I am not suggesting associations that make errors while developing. We all make mistakes. I am talking about those who make irrevocable persuasions. These misfortunes are intentional. Errors, intended to cause you to stumble as you fall.

Good friends contribute to your well-being. They consider the best for you. Their mind forms no contrivance to introduce premeditated negative outcomes. Outcomes, which they know will injure your life. Friends do not attempt to position you in places that will destroy your life. Your best is their sincere interest. They will not entice, nor applaud your destruction, and definitely, not encourage you to play with demons.

Why play games with the devil when you cannot win? When he plays, his grounds for playing are irrevocable consequences for eternal effect. He plays for keeps. Whatever you surrender, you will fight through hell to retrieve it. He has no intent of letting you walk away from what you have allowed yourself to satisfy. His goal is to imprison you, in your own appetite. Therefore, your desires become the bars, which incarcerate you. He will capture you by the thing you lust after the most, and help you destroy yourself in its indulgence.

His undercover and clandestine methods charm your life out of your hands into his. You transfer your authority. He will deceive you to believe you are in control, as you separate from the reality of lost power. The devil uses you against you. Whatever your lust, he deeply drowns you in them without opportunity for you to catch your breath. The kill for him is easy. He will lead you to destroy your own life. He will trick you into believing it is worth it, as you lay down your life for temporary pleasure.

He sedates your conscience with a lie, and turns the lie into your truth. He will cause you to enjoy your incarceration with no desire of freedom. He will persuade you to take ease, enjoy your imprisonment, and gladly accept the penalties of your actions. He will blind you from seeing any reason to be free. You will believe you are having a *hell* of a good time. Lo and behold, "You are."

"Everyone is tempted by his own desires as they lure him away and trap him.

Then desire becomes pregnant and gives birth to sin. When sin grows up, it gives birth to death" (James 1:14-15 GOD'S WORD Translation).

Consider true friendship. Think about relationships supportive of you and your marriage, not associations that undermine and destroy you or your holy union. Not everyone in your life is necessarily someone you should include in your inner circle. Anytime, anyone introduces an idea against your house, your life, or your family; do not continue to lend your ear as their audience. Before you know it, what you hear will influence you, and you may consider something you were so sure you would never entertain.

Influence is a powerful tool. The persuader's motive will determine the direction of influence. Pay close attention to the people who persuade you. Learn to cultivate the company of those who hold a genuine interest in applauding your best. Those who influence you against your own life, you should reconsider them. Use diligence in guarding your ear and heart. It is crucial you protect what enters and flows. Guard your heart and mind to preserve self from being influenced by words, which trip and entangle (Proverbs 4:23-24).

The Scripture names the heart also as the intellectual soul-center of man, in its concrete, central unity, its dynamic activity, and its ethical determination on all sides. All the radiations of corporeal and of soul, life concentrates there and again unfold themselves from thence. The heart is the instrument of the thinking, willing, perceiving life of the spirit. It is the seat of the knowledge of self, of the knowledge of God, of the knowledge of our relation to God, and also of the law of God impressed on our moral nature. It is the workshop of our individual spiritual and ethical form of life brought about by self- activity. The life in its higher and in its lower sense goes out from it. And receives from it the impulse of the direction which it takes; and how earnestly, therefore, must we feel ourselves admonished, how sacredly bound to preserve the heart in purity, so that from this spring of life may go forth not mere seeming life and a caricature of life, but a true-life well-pleasing to God! (From Keil and Delitzsch Commentary on the Old Testament)

Remember the little nursery rhyme; sticks and stones might break my bones, but words will never hurt me. Wars initiate behind words. Be they wars afar off in foreign lands, or private wars in homes in our community. Words are explosive. They can build, and they can teardown the souls of men.

Scripture teaches, "Death and life are in the power of the tongue" (Proverbs 18:21). We can bless with our tongue, and we can curse with it as well. We can calm the human spirit with such a small member, or inflame the soul out of proportion. God framed the world by His Word. The power and influence of words are not something we should take lightly, whether we are using them or listening to them.

By faith, we understand that the worlds were framed by the word of God, so that the things which are seen were not made of things, which are visible (Hebrews 11:3 NKJV).

People can talk people into some amazing predicaments. Especially when they know, it goes against everything they stand for and believe. Nevertheless, it happens repeatedly. Many fall to the power of influence, and become victim. Generations from past to present have proven this truth.

Permissible Adultery

As some couples describe swapping it is the sexual exchange of partners. I call it *'permissible adultery.'* Both the husband and wife permit the adultery. Rules of conduct and code of ethics set by the group govern the permitted conduct. They may swap within their group during a swapping event. However, they cannot swap in secret. In other words, the couple grants permission for the event, beyond that there is no further sexual contact. The couples do not permit independent swap agreements unknown to the husband or wife. If this occurs, the spouse considers this cheating. Imagine that!

"Did it ever occur, or enter the mind of the husband or wife they were taking part in infidelity? Did they consider their breach in marriage? No, they do not consider their conduct…adultery. They agreed to fulfill sexual pleasures, with other like-minded couples, while attesting to the faithfulness of their marriage.

When the husband agreed to surrender his wife to another man, and the wife agreed to lend her husband to another woman, did it not click, each would be committing adultery. Did they not consider they agreed to perform unfaithful acts? Hello! Is anybody home? Now Scripture reads:

> *"But in order to avoid sexual sins, each man should have his own wife, and each woman should have her own husband. Husbands and wives should satisfy each other's sexual needs. A wife doesn't have authority over her own body, but her husband does. In the same way, a husband doesn't have authority over his own body, but his wife does. Don't withhold yourselves from each other unless you agree to do so for a set time to devote yourselves to prayer. Then you*

should get back together so that Satan doesn't use your lack of self-control to tempt you" (1st Co 7:2-5 GW).

Husband and wife should want to fulfill one another's need, and condemn immorality or adultery. They should want to preserve, maintain, and cultivate, not breach their marriage covenant. A marriage covenant is sacred, and the bed is undefiled between husband and wife. Some misinterpret this Scripture to mean; a husband and wife can invite other married couples into their bed to participate in sexual acts, and think voluntary adultery is not defilement. This is far from God's truth. Scripture further teaches:

"Let marriage be held in honor (esteemed worthy, precious, of great price, and especially dear) in all things. And thus let the marriage bed be undefiled (kept undishonored); for God will judge and punish the unchaste [all guilty of sexual vice] and adulterous" (Heb 13:4 Amplified Bible-AMP).

Disclosure

My husband and I were at a dinner engagement with several couples. One couple asked if they could discuss a marital issue. Since we are marriage coaches in our ministry, we agreed to listen. Their conversation was a bit confusing initially; they barraged us with some intense and personal information. As we sat and listened, we finally stopped them to sort through their words. We realized they were swappers.

They were confused, and could not grasp the reality of their spouses leaving them. It was difficult accepting their spouses left them for their swap partners. Neither began healing, nor could they, their hearts craved for the return of their husband and wife. Unfortunately, their spouses divorced them. They sat before us hurt and in pain because their husband and wife swapped them for real, not for an event. The people, with whom they were married, divorced them, and married their swap partners.

The husband of the wife sitting with us filed for divorced, and the wife of the husband sitting with us filed for divorce. The husband and wife of the couple sitting with us wanted divorces to marry their swapping partners. Sadly, they never saw it coming. The shock distressed their heart greatly.

They agreed to participate in devastating and inappropriate relations. After realizing their loss, they also recognized they loved and wanted to save their marriage. However, their decision came too late. The couple seated with us responded to each other's pain, and formed a relationship.

Realizing what they both allowed into their marriage afflicted their soul. They were both horribly shattered. The people they said they loved were gone. They had absolutely no recourse, and no hope of ever reinstating or healing their marriage. It was over! Their life as they knew it…done.

Their spouses fell for the sexual pleasure of their swap partners. They began intimate relations with each other outside of their swap meetings. This couple never believed their spouses would fall for their swap buddies. They did not give a second thought to the possibility of this ever occurring. Sorrowfully, they were sorely remorseful.

"But the man who commits adultery is an utter fool, for he destroys his own soul" (Proverbs 6:32 NLT).

Soul Ties

The husband and wife permitted a soul tie between their spouses and their sexual swapping partners. Failure to consider the consequences or ramifications of such ties severed their own marriage. Never should a woman allow her husband to penetrate another woman. Nor should a husband agree to his wife's penetration of another man. God knits the husband and wife together in one flesh through His marriage covenant. Husband or wife ought not to violate nor disjoin God's union.

"For this reason a man shall leave his father and mother and be joined to his wife, and the two shall become one flesh'; so then they are no longer two, but one flesh. Therefore, what God has joined together, let not man separate" (Mark 10:7-9 NKJV).

A Godly soul tie forms when a husband and wife unite in marriage. Soul ties are more than just a physical union. The tie is spiritual as well (Malachi 2:15 says, *"Has not the LORD made them one? In flesh and spirit, they are His).* The two souls knit together to form one divine union. Marriage is two-souls bound or entwined as one by God. God ties, or merges two souls into one being. The two become one before God in marriage.

There are different kinds of bonds, parents to children, religious community, and friendships. However, for this read, I am sure you understand I am explaining soul ties between a husband and wife. Soul ties develop through permissible sexual intercourse as well as, sexual intercourse unbeknown to either spouse.

When a sensual soul tie develops outside of marriage, it forms an ungodly bond and fragments the soul. The soul is no longer single, but divided. The soul divides with whomever the spouse lends their body.

16 Do you not know that he who unites himself with a prostitute is one with her body? For it is said, "The two will become one flesh" (1 Cor 6:16 NIV).

An ungodly soul tie stimulates thoughts to consider and contemplate the person with whom the soul tied. A soul tie is a dangerous threat to marriage. Instead of a spouse's mind focused on their husband or wife, it divides and lives double. A spouse struggles to aim their full attention toward their husband or wife. The mind, soul, and heart all fluctuates. Scripture teaches; a double-minded man is unstable in all his ways.

[For being as he is] a man of two minds (hesitating, dubious, irresolute), [he is] unstable and unreliable and uncertain about everything [he thinks, feels, decides] (James 1:8 AMP).

The couple before us neglected to consider any consequences. Had they weighted the probabilities, they could have preserved their marriage. As I have heard it said, "Hindsight is 20/20."

The Carnal Appetite

This agreement broke their hearts. It struck soul and spirit, and compelled nothing less than the hand of God to move for them. The souls of these two bruised badly, and their heart still bled profusely. They needed God's loving grace. God alone is the One who will heal the bruised soul, and stop the bleeding heart. The good news; God is willing to heal and restore what seems unsalvageable. He can take our mess, and reconfigure, adjust and align us correctly, if we simply ask. He will help us.

Often, we find ourselves in trouble when blinded by lust, illegal passions, and unhealthy emotions, not to mention the embarrassment following the discovery of our secrets. Passions cannot be one's governing force instead of one's intellect. Too many times, we let our feelings overrule our mind. Our conscious tells us no, but we carry it out anyway. We side with the passion or emotion, and suffer the consequences of not listening to the small voice of wisdom and reason.

Warfare between the mind and the flesh's crave is intense. If the mind does not control the appetite, lust will satisfy its want. When this occurs, lust will injure, hurt, and destroy self, or someone else. Scripture teaches us that our warfare is not carnal. In other words, warfare is a spiritual fight. The fighter fights, in God's knowledge. Knowing God's knowledge is power and victory. The greatest battles we struggle against are the ones in our mind. Thank God for supernatural weapons of warfare.

"For though we walk in the flesh, we do not war according to the flesh, for the weapons of our warfare are not of the flesh, but divinely powerful for the destruction of fortresses. We are destroying speculations and every lofty thing raised up against the knowledge of God, and we are taking every thought captive to the obedience of Christ" (2ⁿᵈ Co 10:3-5 *NASB*).

We live in a world filled with people who have achieved all sorts of degrees. These people influence and encourage other's to do whatever makes them feel good. Often, we neglect the full engagement of our minds to understand a matter's results. If you subscribe to the world's disciplines, they will influence you to do whatever makes you happy. If it feels good, open yourself to its pleasure; just go ahead, do it!

I caution you: passion and conscious will conflict; and without your mind referencing the "Word of God," you will allow what you should avoid. Use your mind for what God created it for, the ability to reason and think, consider a thing and soundly conclude the matter. We allow our emotions, feelings, and passions to run over our intellect, and commit acts against conscious, only to live in the regret of our decisions.

"The heart is more deceitful than anything else and desperately sick—who can understand it?" (Jeremiah 17:9 HCSB)

The thought in a husband's mind of another man being sexually intimate with his wife should be nothing less than appalling, degrading, and loathsome. Nonetheless, people practice and agree with this sort of conduct every day. When a husband allows this violation against his wife, he violates himself. She is as he, one body, and one flesh. The permissible behavior does not protect, defend, or cover the wife. Her heart, soul, and mind are vulnerable and naked. Scripture reads:

> *"The man said: This one, at last, is bone of my bone and flesh of my flesh; this one will be called "woman, for she was taken from man. This is why a man leaves his father and mother and bonds with his wife, and they become one flesh"* Genesis 2:23-24 (HCSB).

A wife's heart should never agree with violating itself to satisfy the immoral acts of a husband. A wife ought never to act against her conscience under any circumstances. God did not instruct her to act against herself. On no account, should she willfully submit to, or tolerate her husband's engagement in sexual relations with another woman.

Unfortunately, we know this happens; I have stories I could share that would topple this one, but why? The results mirror much of the same…a trade in! A wife should never give permission to her husband to penetrate another woman. A husband should never agree to his wife's penetration of another man. It is sexual immorality.

What is Love?

A husband, who is in love, not in like, or in lust with his wife, would never entertain the thought of any man sexually arousing and entering into his bride. The jealously in his heart for what belongs to him will not willingly allow another man's insertion. Not if he is *in* love.

Love does not act or respond like that. Love covers and protects. Love defends and isolates the loved from destructive situations. Love does not devalue or dehumanize the one loved. Genuine love watches and considers what is good for the one loved. Love does not humiliate, embarrass, and commit in the dark what love will not commit in the light. Love does not injure or hurt; it consciously cares. Love is constantly looking forward; thinking of what is always best, plans what is excellent and exercises what is good for the one loved.

"Love is patient, love is kind. It does not envy; it does not boast; it is not proud. ⁵ It does not dishonor others; it is not self-seeking; it is not easily angered; it keeps no record of wrongs. ⁶ Love does not delight in evil but rejoices with the truth. ⁷ It always protects, always trusts, always hopes, always perseveres" (1ˢᵗ Corinthians 13:4-8 New International Version).

I have sat with some women who said, 'if their husband asks them to do something they did not necessarily want to do, but did it anyway; it is their husband's responsibility to God.' Personally, I thought that comment was the most stupid thing I ever heard. I have not found Scripture to support such concepts. It is a matter of teaching.

I will say this, "Scripture is to be read, searched, and studied to find the truth. The truth about what God said." A husband is not accountable for what his wife does in her own body. Nor is the wife responsible for what the husband does in his. Each must stand before God and give an account for their actions.

No one will stand next to anyone. Every person will stand-alone. No one will be able to say to God, "He or she made me do it!" Excuses will not exist, whether thought legitimate or not. Only the truth shall prevail. Every man is responsible to God for his behavior. Everyone will stand before God to give an account for what he has done in his own body.

For we all must appear before the judgment seat of Christ, so that each one may receive the things done through the body, according to what he did, whether good or bad (2ⁿᵈ Corinthians 5:10 NKJV).

Marriage is honorable and everyone ought to regard it. Infidelity is a violation between husband and wife. The two ought to satisfy each another's needs. By no means, is permissible sexual intercourse an activity husbands and wives should practice. Swapping is sexual immorality.

Why agree to violate each other? Sexual violations are acts against one's own body. Since the union of husband and wife are one, they violate each other as well as themselves. The Scripture teaches us in 1st Cor 6:18.

"Stay away from sexual sins." Other sins that people commit don't affect their bodies the same way sexual sins do. A person who commits a sexually sin, actually sins against his or her own body. It is the one sin you charge against yourself. (GW).

Who Can Understand the Grace of God?

Wow! Thank God for forgiveness through our Lord and Savior Jesus Christ. Thank God, He has given us a way to escape such traps and strongholds. Thank God, we have a high priest-Jesus Christ, who we can call on who hears and delivers us from every vice of sexual immorality. Thank God, we possess weapons that are not natural, but are supernatural and powerful.

Thank God for grace and mercy. Thank God, He will come and help us when we call on Him, no matter what our downfall is in life. He will pick us up from the worst of situations and restore our souls whole and healthy again. Thank God, when we do things against ourselves, He has a heart to have pity on us and help us.

Thank God, even in our worst situations He will never turns His back on us. Thank God, He gives us a second, third, fourth and fifth chance. Thank God for His mercy and grace. Thank God for His faithfulness to us. Thank God for extending His hand to us when we call on Him. Thank God, thank God, thank God! Thank God!

God's wisdom is incomparable to ours and capable of leading us through every whim of life. God gave us instruction and counsel concerning sexual immorality. His Word declares the abstinence of it in marriage. Scripture teaches us how to live a whole and healthy married life with our spouses. We must consider the counsel of the One who created and ordained marriage, and His wisdom for upholding it.

Chapter Five

Live In Lover

In my youth, I heard elderly women say, "Why would a man marry you, if he already has his cake and eating it too?" Think about it, "Why marry, if he has the cow, the milk comes free?" They were wise and intelligent women who had learned wisdom through experience. The questions posed made sense, however; I did not consider the answer until many years later.

If a man receives, what he already wants, what is there for him to covet? If a woman surrenders herself to satisfy his needs, honors and respects him as her husband, though he is not, what would challenge him to change his living arrangements? His accommodations are pleasing and rather pleasant from his standpoint. He has what he wants, a faithful lover who conducts herself as his devoted wife...though she is not. For what does he want?

For women who desire marriage, why do they agree with contradicting their own conscience? Why do women commit to a lover's romance and give up all the koochie? Why does she surrender her most beautiful and desirable possession. Knowing that living in this particular fashion does not please her soul.

The heart is an interesting instrument; love, emotions, and feelings influence people to agree against their own conscience. Women grant the room to place themselves in position to move against what they really want. A woman may sincerely want to live with the man she loves. However, she does not necessarily want to live under the condition of a live in lover lifestyle.

I am certain women do not want to think themselves, as a cow, and I make no inference to such. I use the term as an analogy. Nevertheless, let us consider the statement of the older wise women. Does the man not access the milk, as long as he possesses the cow? Have you not heard the phrase, "Possession is nine-tenths of the law?" Do you know what that means? It is an expression meaning ownership is easier to maintain if one has possession of something, and much more difficult to enforce if one does not (Wikipedia).

He is in possession, because she surrendered her ownership. She gave the deed to her property. She handed over her real estate. If he has possession, the ball plays on his court. He can dribble as he chooses, while she surrenders all without enjoying her genuine want.

We know not every man is like this. There are men who earnestly desire his lover for his wife, girlfriend, best friend, and mother of all his children. However, not every woman shares these sentiments. Some women do not care for marriage, just as men do not care for it either. For the woman who does, and contradicts her aspirations, she settles for less, and lives with less than she wants. Outwardly, she might appear satisfied. However, inside, she lives discontented with unfilled desires.

Women give away their life: mind; soul; spirit and body. They give all! Often, the heart runs ahead of reason sprinting to its own injury. Women give, and some become brokenhearted for whatever reason they believed they should have given. How many gave up their real estate in live-in lover relations; hoping to secure a marriage vow, but end up in dissatisfying results?

We can self-inflict madness when wishing to please our own crave or desire. How many decisions have we as women made fully knowing, we should change our mind amid our choice? Even so, we do not. What our heart yearns and craves overthrows our judgment, especially when love seeks a return.

Women are remarkable creatures, and most understand how precious, complete, and invaluable they are. Nonetheless, some still lack identifying their own self-worth. Because of this deficient belief, she devalues her own person. "If she cannot identify her own value as a person, woman, or a human being, she will not see herself as God created her; full of awe and intrigue; significant and necessary.

Even if people can recognize her worth, and significance, often they will not treat her accordingly, because she has not understood her own importance and relevance. This is sad, but true. However, if someone values what is seen, and mentors her to help her become aware of her own significance. She will learn to recognize her own importance and relevance. She will become a self-confident woman, beaming in self-esteem.

Sometimes a man will find himself intimidated by what he notices. Even though he identifies her value, he can also detect her unawareness of her own worth. If he pursues her, in some instances, he will withhold his ability to cultivate what he recognizes. She may appear as a threat to his low levels of self-confidence. It is a sense of safety for him, her remaining blind to her own worth.

Now, on the other hand, a self-confident man will see her for whom she is. He will joyfully aid, promote, and cultivate the greatness he notes within her. He will delight in watching her flourish and blossom into the woman God created within her. She will emerge as a secure and confident woman, and gratefully appreciate him for his unselfish contributions. God knows what he has placed in women and expects them to blossom.

For I know the thoughts that I think toward you, says the LORD, thoughts of peace and not of evil, to give you a future and a hope. (Jeremiah 29:11NKJV)

God's thoughts toward His daughters are deep care and love. He built His daughters to receive ardent affection, understanding, and careful consideration. She is to receive high honor, and mutual respect. The man, who *finds* her, should also find himself overwhelmed with her majesty. Yes, he should discover her. I know this is not popular amongst the current ideologies. Nevertheless, Scripture teaches a man finds…as she prepares herself for his discovery.

She ought not to try to fit herself into the heart of a man who has not prepared himself for her. Proverbs 18; 22 teaches a man who finds a wife finds a good thing and obtains favor from the Lord (HCSB). An unprepared man is not ready to welcome what he has not equipped himself to receive. He will not understand how to handle such a treasure, or express God's affection towards his find. God intends for a man to lavish his wife with love (Ephesians 5:25). A man who understands God's truth agrees with it, and displays extravagant love.

Disguise

Human life is intriguing. Until someone shares their story, you may never know what they have endured. Personal conversations with both men and women, have stunned, shocked, and pleasantly surprised me. The external part of them suggested they were happy and in love, until they sat with me in a corner and decided to talk. I recall one woman in particular expressing grief and disappointment in her live in lover lifestyle.

We were sitting in my office. With her back turned as she sat across from me, she spun around and started talking about her children. A couple minutes into her conversation, her eyes glassed over, and tears were running down her cheeks. I thought, "Oh Lord." I handed her a few tissues to wipe her eyes and dry her nose. She took them and cleaned her face.

She kept dotting the corners of her inner eyes, and said, "I've been living with my boyfriend for the last several years; I keep asking him what he wants, and he isn't telling me anything. I want to get married, but he does not want to marry me. I am living in a secret shame, because I never wanted to live like this." She expressed how embarrassed she was with her live-in lover boyfriend. She explained that she was never comfortable in their live-in lover lifestyle, although it was something she agreed to.

She found herself confused about their relations and lost about what she should do. She had come to believe her lover did not share the same convictions as she did concerning marriage. They lived together for several years. She still waited to hear what he never asked; the most important question in her life. 'Will you marry me?' After all these years, the question never came. Since he chose not to ask her, she considered dissolving their relations. She was heartbroken with the idea of staying, as well as, the notion to leave. She found herself betwixt, in the complexity of emotions.

Her greatest concern was whether she could maintain her lifestyle with only her income. They purchased a home together, and shared the mortgage payment. Her genuine concern was her ability to live the life that she became accustomed to on her own. When I heard her distress, I found myself revisiting a familiar place in my past. Yeah! I remember this all too well; my live in lover experience.

Experience

As I looked at her, I thought about the anxiety I faced with the idea of walking away from it all, as though it was a lot; it was not. In my situation, there was no need for contemplating whether I should stay or leave. It was clear that I needed an exit strategy. Yes, I was very concerned about my finances and stability. However, considering the circumstances, there were no options.

In this stage of life, I was young and immature, and in extreme deep like. Oh yeah, I thought it was love. I believed in something my lover said that I should never have trusted. "I will take care of you." How sweetly those words rang in my ear. Oh my, I have a man who loves me, and has promised to care for me forever. I was mesmerized. I thought this was ideal, a man who wanted to care for me.

My situation was a little different; I was not looking to be married. You see; I was satisfied with the live in lover lifestyle. I had a man who loved me, and I did not mind giving up all. I gave it up for love. Love, I tell you…love. Sadly, one beautiful day without any provocation, reason, or cause; this man, my lover, sat me down. With a very kind, sincere and gentle voice, he said, "I don't need you for anything. I don't need a woman to do anything for me. What a woman can do for me, I can do for myself, and I don't need you; needing a woman is a handicap."

As you can probably imagine, I found myself dumbfounded and crushed. I discovered the meaning of stupefied, as I walked out of the bedroom into the kitchen stumbling in my mind. I walked away without saying a word. Literally, I staggered in my thoughts, as they bounced around in my head. I tried to grasp any form of rational just to understand what he said. I ran through my life with him at a hundred miles an hour trying to catch a grip on what I heard.

I stood frozen over a pot of clam chowder I had on the stove before he asked me into the bedroom. My hand began to stir the soup as I considered every single word. Finally, after I regained my psychological composure, I picked my heart up from the floor and asked myself, "Did you hear what he just said?" He said, 'he does not need you, needing you is a handicap.' I said, "you, speaking to myself, 'are handicapped.'"

Immediately his words made me realize my unknown disability. Now being that I did not choose to remain handicapped, I had to remove my disability. It became apparent that now, at this time in my life, I needed to care for myself. It took a little time to form an exit strategy, but I did. I walked away and never turned around to look back. I decided to begin a new journey of healing and learning how to recapture my worth.

Caught in the Middle

So as I remembered my journey, I clearly understood her predicament. I remember asking myself, "Where am I going? How will I care for myself? She struggled with similar questions. What made her situation more complex were her hopes to marry the man she loved. When the set of circumstances convinced her that he did not intend to marry, she eventually found the courage to do what was right for her. Mutually, they decided he would move into an apartment, which he did.

She said, 'she had attempted to convey what she wanted between the two of them. His initial response was positive, but as time progressed, he showed a lack of interest. He became uneasy when she would initiate a conversation regarding the topic of marriage.' She said, 'If she pressed for clarity concerning his intentions, he would find a reason to avoid the subject. If not able to sidestep the conversation, he would raise issues, which were unrelated. She said, 'it was his way to avoid what she wanted answered.' She said, 'she felt confused, although he would often tell her, he loved her, but resisted telling her of any intent to marry.'

She felt as though she was walking on eggshells. She did not know what to think or believe. Of her own admission, she withdrew her attempts to receive an answer to keep the peace.

When she added the fear of separation into the equation, the thought of happiness walking out the door was definitely not an attractive option. Her fears regulated and managed her conduct to become less forward on the subject. She said she thought, 'why should she mess with a good thing by continuing to press him.'

She let it ride to encourage a pleasant environment within their home. She set her hope aside to restore peace in their relations. Yet, she had no peace of mind. The marital issue remained unresolved, which continued to distress her. Her emotions urged her against her own conscience, knowing it was not what she truly desired. Though she has dreamt of her wedding day, she postpones the idea to secure her live in lover relationship.

Issues of extreme importance eventually rise back to the surface when unresolved. Issues need closure in order to release them and move forward. Later, she addressed him again, conveyed her desire, and questioned his purposes for their future. However, this time in her persistence, she insists he give her an answer.

He told her he cares for and loves her. Nonetheless, he still did not indicate any intent, interest, or plan to marry. She decided to stop living in a cloud of confusion. She said, 'he would not give her an answer about his plans.' She said, "He knows everything else. But, he does not know whether he wants to marry me or not."

What can women do when they find themselves in a predicament that devastates them? How do women spin out from the madness that they contribute to self? When women choose against conscience, their decisions not always result in healthy choices.

You think women would learn from other women's discretions. Some learn, while others do not. I understand each woman chooses her course. However, with so much disposable wisdom, knowledge, and information, women still proceed without caution.

The emotional crave often deceives the heart itself, and women surrender their "real estate" without security. I term it real estate because of the incredible value of a woman's total being. Yet, time and time again, her importance and worth she credits not to her. She esteems the one her heart craves. Yet, his crave, or conviction does not mirror hers.

When I speak of security, I do not speak of financial posturing, although, a husband ought to provide for his wife. I speak of security under the cover of ardent affection. The kind God directed a husband to express toward his wife. However, if a man does not see himself through the eyes of God, as a husband, what is the expectation? If a woman lacks the knowledge of God's idea for herself, how does she measure?

Too often, women yield what they should withhold. Men convince them they are not ready to marry, and women choose to spend their lives waiting. Hoping for that day when he says, "I am prepared to walk down the aisle with you." It may happen, and it may not happen.

Interestingly, I know men who walked down the aisle with someone else. Trust me, when a man cannot fathom his life without his woman, she will not have to wait. He knows he found his "good thing," and he wants not to live without it.

This woman is not alone. Many women have found themselves in similar situations; surrendering their real estate as a down payment of hope in securing a future. Women must remain true to the truth within them. So often, we know better. However, our passion and desire to know love gets the best, of the best of us. God said; "Cast all your burdens on me." When we find ourselves in a pot of pain, God's faithful love will heal us out of it.

Moral of the Story

What is the moral of this chapter? You really have to figure this one out for yourselves. It could be, "Women decide what you want for your own life. If you want marriage, marry. Live the role of a wife, instead of playing the role of one. Why play with what you want. Why commit your soul, mind, and body in hopes of what you desire, when you can live in the reality of what you hope. It very well may not be with the one with whom you were fixated. Let that go. God prepared a husband to find you.

Retain all of yourself for someone who deserves your total surrender. If he wants to marry you, he will. It will not take seven to ten years either. If a man does not want to marry you, he does not want to marry. Be grateful to God you did not talk someone into marriage who really did not want to commit, as your husband. The end of that would be heartbreaking and dreadful.

You must ask yourself the question, "Do I want to play the wife or be the wife?" Why assume responsibilities for a position you do not occupy? Too often, women want to enter into relations prematurely, and end up hurt. Remember, the Scripture notes a *wife* as a good thing (Proverbs 18:22). She is sought, not on the prowl or hunting.

Scripture quotations marked HCSB are taken from the Holman Christian Standard Bible®, Copyright © 1999, 2000, 2002, 2003, 2009 by Holman Bible Publishers. Used by permission. Holman Christian Standard Bible®, Holman CSB®, and HCSB® are federally registered trademarks of Holman Bible Publishers.

Chapter Six

Hush

ooking from past to present, it appears women have found a place of independence. Today women are more resilient and vocal about decisions and choices affecting their lives. Many women learned how to stand for what she believes, and is comfortable voicing her position. Whatever the conviction, women no longer restrain themselves from expressing their mind.

Women have made an indelible mark in their plight to make their voices heard, as well as demanding respect. We live in the twenty-first century, and think all is well, but is it? The female gender has traveled a great distance, but we cannot place a stake in the ground and claim we have arrived. As long as there are women whose voices remain unheard, the plight continues.

For so many years, women learned silence through some of the most horrific trails and hardships in life. They did not speak of the abuses they incurred, mainly because of fear and humiliation. The attached disgrace and shame associated with the instances placed its hand over women's mouths.

The humiliation and embarrassment of someone knowing their abuse often weighed heavier than the reality of the surreptitious acts of assault. Too often, women believed the mistreatment would eventually stop. With love as well as kindness, they held to the belief, the ill-treatment would pass with time. They held hold to hope believing that one day it would get better.

Sadly, men exercised violence to fixate fear and intimidation in the heart of women. Intimidation served to humiliate the soul, which wrought lack of self-esteem, embarrassment, and absence of self-worth. Women learned to *hush* during mistreatment to survive. They learned how to suffer affliction and heartache without uttering a single word to anyone.

Somehow, their fear trickled down from generation to generation and from house-to-house. They taught on lookers how to suffer quietly. They endured through real and imminent threats of harm. It did not matter what age: creed; race; color, or economical or social status. All women seemed affected.

A woman's silence was not her greatest ally. Her silence proved to be her greatest enemy against the health of her body, soul, and spirit. Silence proved an enemy to her body, because she covered the ruthless offenses continued against her. Silence proved an enemy to her soul, as the threat of constant fear clouded her right to see her liberty and freedom. It proved an enemy to her spirit, because it lay troubled, broken, and wounded. Nevertheless, if her cry pierced through the windowpane, no one would run to her rescue. Who would come to her aide? After all, she is just a woman.

I remember living in an apartment complex as a young woman, and listening to a woman scream as her husband beat her. The sound of her cries rang clear. I could hear them piercing through her apartment into ours. I walked toward the noise and laid my ear against the living room wall. I listened to every cry. Nobody came to her rescue. I assumed he stopped beating her, because I no longer heard her yell. I walked to the front door and peeked toward her entrance, but she did not emerge. I expected the police to arrive. No one ever came, no police, no help, and no rescue team. I did not know what to think, or do, except hope she was alive.

Women wore and still wear invisible masks perpetrating fake smiles without anyone noticing. They cover up well. If others detected or sensed discomfort, they might ease over and quietly ask, "Are you ok," while looking behind them to ensure no other eyes witnessed their concern. Of course, if identified as a meddler in another's personal affairs, she too might suffer repercussions.

Women cared about women. Nonetheless, some were afraid to help. Therefore, women learned to *hush* and suffer in silence. If she found a confidant to share and voice her problem, the confidant could only lend her shoulder as a support to cry on. Usually, during these times, the confidant reluctantly advised her to try to make the best of a bad predicament.

Not often did she receive an offer to leave, because the abuser would seek and find her. This limited her ability to run for any significant time or distance. Where could she go without discovery? Once discovered, she returned to suffer the consequences of an attempted escape.

Brave women did stand to aid those women without courage and strength to stand on their own. However, the guilty convinced them with hope-filled promises to come back. Women returned home. They placed themselves at risk enduring the same set of circumstances.

Many women suffered at the hand of the one entrusted to protect and care for her. She bore the weight of embarrassment instead of the causative husband, shouldering his disgrace. Women covered the ill-treatment to protect the responsible from public humiliation while they lived in undisclosed shame. They protected the guilty hands of all sorts of men, in all different shades of color, and varied positions of occupations, the intellectual, as well as men who lacked common sense.

Women have covered the cheater: the physical abusive; the sexual assaulter; the condescending; the arrogant; the tyrant and the liar. Yet, they remained attached to these men. Some women remained because she saw no other choice. Some women stayed because they feared for their safety. Many women committed their hearts to love in spite the difficulty.

When a woman marries, she trusts the man with whom she stood before God to keep her safe. She has every confidence he will protect her. She does not marry with the preconceived notion that she will not receive his love, consideration, and care. God created her to want fulfillment of such affections. The deep-seated need to receive love, and longing for protection and care from the one with whom she has given herself. She does not give herself anticipating fear, or neglect. On the other hand, she surrenders herself expecting to thrive in the liberty that love promotes.

Still Endangered

It is interesting to talk about past occurrences. However, when past incidents live and thrive today, we find history is not so far behind us. In fact, it is on our heels. How did we come to this travesty of abuse against women? Moreover, why does this issue still exist? You ask, "What issue?" The issue I call the "*hush*" syndrome. Yesterday women silenced themselves, for multiple reasons. Today we discover they still do.

My husband and I conversed with a couple who decided to leave a church. The knowledge of repeated abuse by one of their pastors left them distressed. The behavior of the pastor primarily shaped their decision for wanting to leave. They found themselves amid an uncomfortable and unacceptable quandary…the involvement of a pastor who beats his wife. The disregard for the pastor's wife, as well as the lack of discipline imposed upon the pastor's behavior became troubling.

The pastor's wife landed on their doorstep one evening asking for help. Just beaten by her husband, she feared for her safety. She sought refuge in their home. They brought her into their house to comfort and try to protect her. After several hours of talking about what occurred, her husband spoke with her by phone. After a considerable time of speaking with him, she unwillingly returned home at his request.

They stated two reasons for their frustration: The assaultive behavior of the pastor, and the senior pastor of the church allowing him to retain his position. In addition, the church did not want the wife of the assaultive pastor to say anything. She needed to *hush* regarding the matter.

Her quietness would not expose her husband's abuse. In this way, he could keep his position as pastor. She was to tell no one about the incident and encouraged to suffer quietly to prevent any embarrassment to her husband. Other staff members directed the couple to remain silent as well, and not expose the pastor's indiscretions.

When they inquired of her well-being after returning home, she acted as if nothing occurred. According to the couple, what troubled them the most were staffers' knowledge of the pastors' behavior and the ministry not taking disciplinary action against him. Those who knew turned their head as though nothing happened. The couple said they addressed the issue on several occasions, but to no benefit. After the last incident, they were so frustrated they wanted no further involvement with their church.

It should be an uncommon occurrence for women to suffer violence in church. However, it happens. What is worst is when people in positions in the church are the abusers. No, it should not happen, but it does. It is unacceptable and intolerable behavior. No one should continue to hold any position in ministry who abuses his or her family. I included women as well, unbelievably; some of them are abusers also. Violence misrepresents the heart of God.

Hardened Hearts

What happened in man's heart toward women? What has caused the hardening? Men must examine their heart and answer the question individually, although not all are guilty. For the innocent this scenario need not apply. Nevertheless, for those who are, "How did you fall into this mental and emotional deficit?" It is a fall and not a stand, because God does not uphold this kind of treatment toward his daughters.

After all, God built woman from Adam's rib and flesh (Genesis 2:23). He created her to benefit from the protector from which she came. God took part of man for the express purpose of building him a helpmate. "God built woman from the same identical flesh and bone of man. She is of the same nature. Yet, she differs in physical characteristics, shares in equal powers, faculties, and rights (Adam Clark).

God through His extraordinary skill structured woman as man's perfect reflection of self. When man saw woman he recognized himself in her. At last, someone who is as I am. God created her for an inseparable unity and fellowship with man. For God said, "It is not good that the man be alone" (Gen 2:18-22). "*Of such a help the man stood in need, in order that he might fulfill his calling, not only to perpetuate and multiply his race, but to cultivate and govern the earth*" (*Keil* and Delitzsch Commentary).

"By this the priority and superiority of the man, and the dependence of the woman upon the man, are established as an ordinance of divine creation. This ordinance of God forms the root of that tender love with which the man loves the woman as himself, and by which marriage becomes a type of the fellowship of love and life, which exists between the Lord and His Church (Eph. 6:32). If the fact that the woman was formed from a rib, and not from any other part of the man, is significant; all that we can find in this is, that the woman was made to stand as a helpmate by the side of the man" (Keil and Delitzsch Commentary).

God never asked, or directed His daughters to position their bodies for abuse. He did not declare them a punching bag for man. He built woman from man as a more fragile and delicate vessel. He built her to assist him, and ultimately complete him. God returned Adam's rib as his help.

Woman does not labor as man, for God did not create her for such laborious and strenuous task. She physically tires more easily. Yet, she is weaker, not in spirit, mind, or application of thought, but in physical potency. God built her to converse, share her mind, Godly wisdom, and help man rule.

God assembled, formed, and created woman as a: companion; complement; help, and best friend. Since, God made the husband and wife one flesh, "What man does against his wife, he does against himself." Through the unity of the marriage covenant, God made them one. How many men and women understand God's principle?

Understanding God's idea is an endless treasure to men and women alike who want to grasp the oneness between husband and wife. Some men have grown and developed into more understanding husbands by God's Spirit and wisdom. However, because of the continuing physical and psychological ill-treatment of women, many still lack wisdom about marital relations and do not understand God's expected response to their wives.

Therefore, wives suffer from emotional bankruptcy. The wisdom and understanding necessary of a husband to support and uphold her greatly lacks.

Husbands, in a similar way, live with your wives with understanding since they are weaker than you are. Honor your wives as those who share God's life-giving kindness so that nothing will interfere with your prayers (GOD's WORD®, 1ˢᵗ Peter 3:7).

In the House

Some years ago, I attended a Christian conference in California. In the conference auditorium, a couple stood alongside me. I overheard the wife graciously ask her husband about what to do. It is interesting, because I honestly do not recall his words, but I remember his vocal tone and disposition. I have yet to forget the tone in which he spoke, or his posture, slightly elevated and impatient.

He walked away and left her standing in the middle of the auditorium. Perhaps he caught my attention, not so much, by what he said, but by his reaction to her question. I remember the expression on his face, un-relaxed, almost as though she bothered him.

I felt compassion for her. I did not say anything. I did not think I needed to. I should have because it bothered me. She did not see me looking at her. She looked confused in the moment. I could only infer such as she appeared mentally absorbed. Besides, I was not trying to appear visible, even though I kept my eye on her. She stood there for a few moments and finally moved about the crowd.

People really do not realize how often other people notice them. I am sure she probably thought no one paid attention. Was she embarrassed? "I do not know." Something happened inside.

Her facial appearance said it did. It showed briefly before she masked it over.

I learned that people are comfortable in public doing what they practice privately at home. Underlying behaviors sometimes slip, and at times, they arise unintentionally. Was this just a glitch in his behavior? I do not know. She did not appear comfortable, or at ease. She appeared lost, anxious, and not knowing what to do.

Have you watched children when they visit? During the visit, the child runs rampage through your home, while the parent relentlessly tries to manage the child's conduct. The child is comfortable acting out the behavior displayed in their home. When parent and child visit, the child just does what the child normally does; run amok all over the place. So I would guess, he like the child, responded to his own normality.

This may not seem worth mentioning. However, I believe it is. Besides, the expression on her face was memorable. She did not respond, she did not say a word as he walked away. Her mouth may not have uttered anything, but her face spoke on her behalf, 'I am hurt.'

Any behavior non-reflective of God's heart toward a wife from her husband ought not to be! Yet, it is in the church *house*. There are women sitting in God's house hurting. These women not all suffer physically. They suffer physiologically and emotionally as well. Their minds are distressed and their emotions are unstable. They live under the roof with a spouse who chooses not to talk, is condescending, speaks to them as though their ideas are stupid, devalues them, and restricts his love and support.

This is an uncomfortable subject matter. One that needs attention, but nobody wants to talk about it. Nevertheless, we must. Let us not turn our heads as though it does not exist, because it does. I coach women who feel so empty, insignificant, and unimportant. Their words do not count; their weaknesses not acknowledged; and their husbands do not see them as the woman God created. Women and wives are in need of healing. The only way to begin the process is to acknowledge it exist, and talk about resolution through understanding God's idea of woman, wife and marriage.

We who are in the house ought not to conduct ourselves like the people who are on the outside. We have the answers. We hold the mysteries. Nevertheless, if we ourselves do not acknowledge the answers or respect the truth, how great is our deception? If we disregard so great an instruction how can we live in the fullness of what Scriptures teaches and the grace God provides? We possess life in abundance. We have abundant understanding and wisdom, both of which are natural and spiritual.

Christ is God's mystery in whom is hidden all treasures of wisdom and knowledge. The faithful acquire access to treasures of wisdom and knowledge to which the faithless have no privilege. Through Christ, we possess riches of assured understanding. Let the faithful not be deceived with persuasive or empty arguments. Let us be careful and not become captive through philosophical ideologies predicated on human traditions. The traditions established on the elemental forces of the world, and not founded upon God's living Word.

God grants us grace, and in His grace, He heals and replenishes our soul to live a life that is consistent with His passion for us. A life full of the provisions He has lavished on both husband and wife equally to enjoy. If we provide refuge to the one who is erred, and hide behavior, while women are dying, physically and emotionally, how can either benefit from the health and restoration of soul that God graciously provides?

How can the only One who can do such a magnificent work heal, if we act as though the issues do not exist? The one who covers hidden things for the one whom he knows is wrong, and sanction him regardless, because of the threat of shame if exposed, is as guilty as the one he allows to hide behind his authority. So how can all obtain healing, if the behavior remains covered in

God's house? God wants our soul and marriages whole and full of spiritual and natural health and vitality.

We ought not to continue to hide behavior that does not correspond with God's Word. The promises of God are for both man and woman alike. God has not prejudiced His Word. We are joint heirs to the goodness: grace, blessings, and Kingdom of God. I know we all have issues, we must contend with in the dust we live. Nevertheless, let us at least put forth the effort to grow into the Word God entrusted with us to live.

Submit to God, not to ideologies of the world; or gender-specific traditions of men or women. Neither to teaching that is inconsistent with Scriptural truths. What has God the Father said, period! We adhere to and continue in the Word of truth. As a result, son and daughter receive the fullness God ordained for both to enjoy richly.

Those joined in holy matrimony, "in the name of the Lord Jesus Christ," glorify God in response and treatment toward each other. God created marriage, and He has given us the recipe of how to cultivate and sustain it. If we do what we choose; disregard each other; God is not glorified, and *we* are not satisfied. Our marriages can be healthy if we chose to follow God's prescription. Have we really looked, or have we neglected the study of Scripture to know the truth?

Diminished Capacity

Somewhere, something drastically erred in life toward the lesser and more fragile vessel God built for man. It seemed to have become an epidemic…the mistreatment of the fetus caring gender. Yes, women have come a long way in fighting for their rights and treatment, and are justified in the fight. However, the "hush" epidemic still exists.

You would think since it has been more than two thousand years ago since Christ's appearance, we would have improved. To some degree, we have, but it is just a degree, and it is not significant enough. It is intolerable when husbands publicly disrespect their wives. When this occurs, she suffers public humiliation. Where is the application of God's Word in a man's heart toward his wife?

In the ancient of days, women had no regress if their husbands treated them without love, honor, and respect. Men's hearts became harsh, hard, and cold toward not only their wives, but also the female gender. From the Garden of Eden until the time of Moses, man's heart digressed toward their wives as well as women in general. Sadly, "Some remain stuck in ideologies and traditions, instead of illuminating their minds in the truth of God's Word."

Due to the hardness of a man's heart, Moses' allowed men to give their wives a letter of divorcement, but Jesus said, "From the beginning it was not so" (Matthew 19:8). So how did men remove themselves so far from the original manuscript of God's will for the union He created between a man and woman? It is because of the lust of flesh, and the appetite for sin.

When God sent Christ, He reinstated God's original concept: one man, one woman, joined in holy matrimony before God as one flesh. Christ restored God's genesis for the marriage covenant. Some may choose to abide in the traditions and allowances of old. We as the people of God do not live in the prehistoric, but the new and living way.

Christ died to not only redeem us to a right relationship with God and return us to a holy relationship with Him; He also healed our soul from sickness and disease, and cleansed us from the pollutants of our past.

Christ has graced us with another chance to see life through the mind of God with understanding, and not through the passions of our own flesh. These passions perpetuated and perplexed our soul to become sick in the first place. We pursued what was destructive to our own existence, instead of heeding the Word of God, which satisfies. It upholds, and sustains the health of every human soul. So now, for a short while, we have opportunity once again to listen.

Let us take advantage of the opportunity to see the treatment of the wife through the eyes of Scripture, and live in the abundance of what God ordained for good. A wife should never live in the threat of fear for her safety. A husband should always work hard to ensure his wife knows she is secure. I am not solely referring to the tangible security, but beyond the house. The security of a touch; safety in a sound; beauty in a response; all surrendered in the most precious way through passionate love coupled with Godly understanding.

Gen 2:18-22 Electronic Database. Copyright © 1996 by Hendrickson Publishers, Inc. Used by permission. All rights reserved.

MATTHEW HENRY'S COMMENTARY ON THE WHOLE BIBLE New Modern Edition Complete and Unabridged in Six Volumes. Electronic Database. Copyright © 1991 by Hendrickson Publishers, Inc. Used by permission. All rights reserved.

CLARKE'S COMMENTARY Electronic Database. Copyright © 1996, 2003 by Biblesoft, Inc. Used by permission. All rights reserved.

KEIL & DELITZSCH COMMENTARY ON THE OLD TESTAMENT NEW UPDATED EDITION Electronic Database. Copyright © 1996 by Hendrickson Publishers, Inc. Used by permission. All rights reserved.

Scripture is taken from GOD'S WORD®, © 1995 God's Word to the Nations. Used by permission of Baker Publishing Group.

Cite This Article: Eager, George B. "Husband, International Standard Bible Encyclopedia. Edited by James Orr. Blue Letter Bible. 1913. 5 May 2003 3July 2011.

<http://www.blueletterbible.org/Search/Dictionary/viewTopic.cfm?type=GetTopic&Topic=Husband&DictList=4#ISBE>

"Is there a human being," asks Socrates", with whom you talk less than with your wife?"

Chapter Seven

Daughters

$\mathcal{L}$ ife is full of interesting people. The more you talk to people you grow in understanding life, and why people react or respond they way they do. My husband and I dined at a friend's bistro. As we sat outside enjoying the summer night, a young woman joined our table. It just so happened we were discussing this book.

After listening for a few minutes, she asked the name of the book. I responded, "Why Did You Give Up The Koochie and Now You Mad." Amused, she let out a big shout and thrust forward laughing. When she sat up she said, "You know my mother never taught me it was worth anything. I never knew the value of it until I became pregnant. She did not teach me it meant anything important. So I didn't care about it at all!"

We sat surprised by what she said. In essence, she never esteemed herself as valuable. Unfortunately, she had not learned the value of herself. Her statement captivated the moment. She did not laugh while she spoke. She made an honest, real, and pure statement. I thought, "She is not alone. How many young women believe likewise?"

What happened to mothers who taught daughters how to become young women? Besides, what happened to fathers who taught daughters their significance? What happened to teaching them the importance of the gift they are from God to humanity? When did mother and father stop teaching daughters how to preserve themselves? Daughters should know how to safeguard self for the man who will inquire of her hand, instead of asking for her whole body. She needs education regarding the attributes men ought to possess long before his approach.

So many young women become disillusioned after they give up their prized possession. They do not understand their value as a whole person. They lack understanding their own self-worth, which sabotages their self-esteem.

The impact of madness occurs in the reality of truth. The force of truth can mess you up, especially, when truth is a negative. Negative truth, is truth women learn the hard way. It is not that truth is negative, in and of itself, absolutely not. The hardship in the lesson learned that truth exposed becomes the negative. Not the truth itself, but the grievous experience endured in light of the truth.

The age of a woman matters not. However, for the inexperienced it is quite devastating. When young women surrender themselves, and men treat them without value, the experience bruises the heart tremendously. The pain can, and sometimes does last a lifetime.

This pain, which results in madness, is not ordinary madness. This madness does not come from insanity, or anger. It is psychological and emotional trauma tee-tar-tottering between humiliation and ignorance. The heart and mind suffers anguish naked to the eye, which scrapes and scars the soul. The invisible wounds show up in attitude, character; conduct; self-esteem; and faith.

Many young carry the weight of what they allowed in their lives from their past. They wrestle with the fear and regret of what they allowed. Often they struggle with forgiveness of self as well. After wrong decisions, their hearts end up wounded, as they face the consequences of choice.

Young women face many challenges when surrendering themselves without considering the outcome, yet, so many do. With young and old women, they want love. They desire attention and affection from their male counterpart. Emotionally and psychologically, young women are not ready or prepared for what their immature hearts want. Often, they are too impatient to wait and learn to date responsibly. Yes, there is such a thing as responsible dating...not crossing the line. Which line? The invisible line established by God's principles. When immature or mature step over the principle line, it usually causes one to disrespect self.

Young women have amazing willpower and it often moves them to invite prematurely what their hearts are not prepared to handle. Yet, their hearts are not reluctant to wait, so they pursue what they feel. When Pandora's Box opens, they cannot control what comes out. They throw discipline and conscious to the wind, as their emotions twist and turn in the moment.

Submitting their bodies cost their freedom. They did not consider pregnancies, sexual transmitted diseases, or the need to continue their education. These young women face a lot of pressure. Not to mention, the thought of others finding out what they have done.

They deal with the emotional fear associated with telling a parent. The psychological aspects of what people will think, as well. So often, we see young women face their fears alone. Boys and men have fun at the cost of a young woman's heartache. Many, many times their heartthrob disappears like vapor.

Repeatedly, we watch the results of choices by our youth. We do not have to look too far; they are right in our houses. These issues arise within our own families and we find them disheartening when they occur. We understand how their choice will affect the rest of their lives. We see the lack of training, skill, and ignorance. Yet; they believe we are the ones who know nothing about what we advise.

We find many youths do not care to listen to the sound instruction of their parents or elders. They do not realize how wealthy their parents are with a bank full of wisdom from which they can draw. We understand they need our wisdom even when they do not. Nevertheless, many youth think considering a parent's instruction is senseless.

With age and experience comes wisdom. Youth possess neither. Even if they are scholastically smart and intelligent, they lack real life experience. Nonetheless, they believe they know more than the aged. Sooner than later, you need to extend your shoulder. They live to learn they do not know everything. Life happens, and the counsel of wise parents becomes necessary.

Many young women believe in a need for intimate relationships at such a young age. They want involvement in relations without much thought about the outcome. Their immaturity affects their long-range vision for their future. The want is for the present-day. They want what they want right now. Preparation takes too long; life is in the moment, because life is right now. They hurry, missing important instructions to help them mature.

Dreams, goals, and ambitions are not attractions they set for their future. The current thought process impedes their ability to think any further than the present moment. The intentional pursuit or drive for future preparation is not a motivating factor. I heard Bishop Hooks say, "People sacrifice their future on the altar of the immediate." "They forfeit their future for the desire of the day."

Remember those high school years; remember "The one?" You know the one you thought you wanted; the one you could die for everyday of the week. Have you seen *the one* lately? Glad you did not die for that one, hum. As life processed you, you realized they were not worth dying for anymore.

However, an immature mind has difficulty processing the truth. They do not know they will probably change the way they think in a few years. However, if this is 'what I feel' today, 'what I feel' will last forever. Nothing else makes sense except what their heart believes for the present moment. They do not see beyond where they are. They act, as though this is it. Time has a way of maturing us. When it does, we no longer consider the stuff we once did. Well, maybe some of us do not!

Father Teach

A young woman's mind is gullible to the influential voices spoken to it. When innocent young women hear men compliment their beauty, she likes what she hears. It is nice to receive compliments. However, she need not become euphoric because she has received them. Most do, as compliments stroke and tap on emotions.

It is not necessary for young women to hear someone else tell them they are beautiful. I am not suggesting expressions of admiration be withdrawn, or not given. I believe positive remarks are necessary, they boost the human spirit and inspire the soul. However, when the father establishes within his daughter her beauty, she does not become flabbergasted behind receiving credit for her splendor. Daddy already confirmed-God created her beautiful! Daughters need daddy's confirmation. That way, when Jack, Jim, or Johnny Frank wants to whisper some sweet notion, she retains her stability.

How often are young women intrigued by the words of adolescent or older men? Men sideswipe women through conversation all the time. Men bait with a little conversation here, a calculated remark there, and an attractive smile to soften the catch. They use words to tickle the ear, and leave a delicate print in the innocent mind. A mind untrained and unsophisticated in life's affairs.

Often, these expressions of praise and regard influence many young women into relations their tender hearts cannot handle. However, they choose to indulge in them anyhow, neglecting the advice of mature people. 'What do old people know anyway? They talk about stuff; they went through a long time ago. What do they know about what is going on today?'

Of course, our counsel to them is so old fashion. A young mind appears remarkable and brilliant, but remains an underdeveloped instrument for such costly ventures. The mature clearly understand; the players change, but the game stays the same. So the inexperienced mind gambles into unfamiliar territory without any counsel to their regret.

I believe when a daughter hears her fathers' reassuring convictions of her beauty, as well as declarations of who she is; it will make all the difference in the world; instead of a stranger affecting her world by a compliment. If dad already assures her and helps build her confidence, when she hears words contrary to what daddy taught, she will respond differently.

She will appreciate he noticed; however, she will not emotionally stumble over it. When she already knows how beautiful she is, what could a strange voice tell her? She knows her father loves her, covers and protects her. Her response would be, "I know I am beautiful; is there anything else you recognize within me?" It probably would catch him off guard, and he would probably think she thinks too much of herself. She should think much of herself. God designed woman to be just that astonishing and confident.

During the writing of this book, I held a seminar and invited women of various age groups and ethnicities. A young woman age twenty-two read this chapter. When she finished reading, she said, "I didn't have a father to tell me I was beautiful. I did not have a father to teach me those things. The person that I heard tell me I was beautiful was the pastor at my church. He has been a father figure."

Many fathers have never helped build their daughters into sound, strong, and courageous women. Girls grow up handicapped emotionally, because they needed the stability of their father's love and assurance. Being daddy's girl is a dream instead of a real experience.

Thank the Lord for men who love God and esteem women. When they compliment, their true intent is to build that woman's confidence in her. They see behind the smile into her wounded spirit. Because she is broken, the love of God in him chooses to encourage, uplift, and build her to understand and believe in the woman God created her to know. He encourages her to recognize her potential, and develop into the God woman within her. He promotes her pursuit of greatness.

Women young and old are marvelous and spectacular creatures. Women ought to know how wonderfully crafted they really are by God. When women recognize their own beauty, they will not be intrigued or mesmerized by frivolous words. Women will expect a man to identify the beauty within her. She will anticipate he recognize the significance within her authored and sanctioned by God.

I have always believed that a father should teach his daughter about the expectations of men. Since he is a man and thinks as one, he can direct her mind; guide her heart in what qualities and attributes she should consider; and why she should carefully ponder them.

A father should teach her how her husband should love, provide and protect her (Ephesians 5:25). First by his pattern as a husband, so she knows by example. He should illustrate how a man should treat a lady in his home. Therefore, she has a gauge to measure how her husband should handle her. She can look at her father and say, "Daddy you taught me well."

> *25-28Husbands, go all out in your love for your wives, exactly as Christ did for the church—a love marked by giving, not getting. Christ's love makes the church whole. His words evoke her beauty. Everything he does and says is designed to bring the best out of her, dressing her in dazzling white silk, radiant with holiness. And that is how husbands ought to love their wives. They're really doing themselves a favor— since they're already "one" in marriage.*

> *29-33No one abuses his own body, does he? No, he feeds and pampers it. That's how Christ treats us, the church, since we are part of his body. And this is why a man leaves father and mother and cherishes his wife. No longer two, they become "one flesh." This is a huge mystery, and I don't pretend to understand it all. What is clearest to me is the way Christ treats the church. And this provides a good picture of how each husband is to treat his wife, loving himself in loving her, and how each wife is to honor her husband* (The Message MSG, Ephesians 5-25-33).

A woman can instruct her regarding her feminine care. She can teach her well-mannered characteristics on becoming a young woman. She can show her how to care for her body, counsel her to conquer her emotions and use her mind. In addition, she can teach her about managing her house and all the responsibilities that come alongside that duty. However, daddy can teach how to guard her heart. He can raise her awareness concerning the falsities of masculine deceptions. He can teach her why she ought to preserve herself for the one who deserves everything she contains.

> ³ *In the same way, older women are to be reverent in behavior,*
> *not slanderers, not addicted to much wine. They are to teach*
> *what is good,* ⁴ *so they may encourage the young women to love*
> *their husbands and to love their children,* ⁵ *to be self-controlled,*
> *pure, homemakers, kind, and submissive to their husbands, so*
> *that God's message will not be slandered* (Titus 2:3-5 HCSB).

How awesome the challenge for fathers to give their daughters something to reach for. He can help her conceive appropriate expectations, so when Bozo the Clown comes around she will not trip and fall for his nonsense. His guidance will raise her awareness in distinguishing the difference between sensibility and stupidity. In this way, she can guard her heart to prevent forming senseless decisions based on futile rhetoric.

She needs daddy as an example in her home, so when she leaves, she can identify what is good and decent opposed to what is not. It is necessary for her to observe her father model himself as a man and husband (Colossians 3:19). As a father he is the first male figure she identifies with and trusts. He can educate her on how to recognize and trust the right things. Throughout her life, the foundation of his counsel provides a solid platform on which she can stand.

> *Husbands, go all out in love for your wives. Don't take*
> *advantage of them* (Colossians 3:19 MSG).

It will cause awareness in her that she would not otherwise possess. It will equip her to gauge her choices and consider consequences more appropriately. What a father teaches and speaks into his daughter's life is extraordinary. A father's participation is priceless. His spoken words of wisdom will last her for the rest of her life.

Fathers, invest your time, counsel, and wisdom into your daughters, because they desperately need your guidance, your time, and your love. We think boys need so much from their fathers, but daddy's girls need as much if not more from their father's presence.

Great dads have developed many strong and confident women. I applaud you for every word you have seeded into your daughter's life. Your care and consideration voiced through your words will resonate throughout her life. You elevated her ability to assess relations through your Godly counsel.

For dads who invested their heart. You developed a stronger and much wiser woman. She will credit the impartation of your love and wisdom to her account. I am certain she is grateful to God for you in her life, and most of all; being her dad, a father who participates.

Chapter Eight

Giving up The Koochie

As new ideas emerge over time, people's minds change. Life experiences collect information that expands our knowledge and contributes to the future of our life. Lessons learned from experiences challenge us to evaluate life more closely. Experienced information produces more intelligent and rational choices; you would think!

Experience has a way of educating your life, like no other teacher. Whether good or bad experiences, they teach the importance of making sound decisions. Life produces experience; experience wisdom; and wisdom tells you what you should and ought not to do. One's life should reflect progression not regression. However, new ideas produce controversial mindsets.

When observing the attitudes of women a dramatic change in concept of lifestyle has emerged. Ideas most women would never tolerate or accept, today they embrace. For instance, the idea of a woman saving herself for her wedding day has changed. A woman who holds true to this idea, stands her ground, and chooses not to let a man prematurely lie between her legs has become somewhat of a stigma.

If a woman reaches thirty years old and she declined to let a man discover her pleasure, society frowns on her as old fashion. Society shouts, 'what is wrong with you.' Progressive and secular ideas persuade women to believe something is wrong with her, if she protects her virginity. It has become almost shameful for a young woman to consider withholding herself until asked to marry.

Every immature or mature woman controls her own body. For the woman, she owns her most sacred treasure until the moment; she surrenders her precious jewel to the one she chooses to share her life. Here is the problem; most women allow the robbery of their precious treasure. New ideas and concepts convert what they believe and conform their mind to present ideologies.

Contrary to Godly influence, society's ideas will cause you to regret, what you do, for the rest of your life. If a woman will not stand for what she believes, and falls to her influence, she will find herself heartbroken. She cannot live by a set of thoughts contrary to God's idea for her.

Unfortunately, some women today give out koochie like throwing out the trash. No care or regard for their body. It is sad to say however true; we live in a generation that believes; if they practice anal or oral sex, they are preserving themselves for someone special. How deceptive the idea. They think by not engaging in vaginal sexual intercourse, purity is preserved.

Many young women believe that if they allow their boyfriends to sodomize them, they save their virginity. Young women think they preserve one part of their body while tainting another. The worst deception is self-deception. Many young women think if she surrenders her rectum, she will preserve her vagina. She lacks understanding that she defiles her whole body. She allows sexual acts that taint and soil her purity.

> *Stay away from sexual sins. Other sins that people commit don't affect their bodies the same way sexual sins do. People who sin sexually sin against their own bodies (1ˢᵗ Corinthians 6:18 GOD'S WORD).*

Sodomy is not the only allowed offense. Oral sex contends for first place. Young women wrap their mouths around someone's private structure, as another method to preserve or save her virginity. As long as vaginal sex does not occur, young women believe they retain their purity. Sadly, after allowing such offenses they deceive self to believe such nonsense.

When did it become wrong for a woman to want to keep herself anyway? Society will criticize a woman for doing so. Has she no choice? Of course, she does, but according to societal standards, she should open her legs and give of herself. To wait on her husband is a foreign idea. New ideas tell women, 'You do not need to do that anymore.' If she waits to long to experience sexual intercourse, something must be wrong with her.

We live in a perverse time. What most women frowned on, as disgraceful behavior for men, they now repeat. You see it more and more in young people; let us have sex for the fun of it. Somewhere preservation lost its value. The value, especially for women, is becoming worthless.

Many frustrated and mad women walk around heartbroken. Most think madness is anger, but madness is a condition or state of being. Women's hearts have melted and their souls are sick, because they gave up too much too soon. Yielding themselves resulted in embarrassment. Women gave birth to children men did now want. They gave their heart to men who trampled on it. Women surrendered their bodies to men who did not care one bit for them. Numerous women are mad because they act like men, yet never receive the respect of them.

Women have become mad over choice and consequence. Mad, because nothing feels good about feeling used; even when they believe they are the one using. Women will never satisfy self when embracing man's attitudes. God did not create her soul for disfiguring. He created her for love, nurturing, and care. Absent these things, her soul lacks what God created it to receive. For that matter, God neither intended a man to mar his own soul by sexual deviance either.

I do not think women traded love and respect for a moment of sexual disrespect. I think they want equal playing rights. Equal playing rights places women on the same courts as men; playing the same foolish games, only to their own hurt. Men own no playing rights; they never have. Until women understand this, they give all their rights away.

Women need to understand God's idea about them. They need to realize what He said about who they are. Once she realizes God's idea of her, she will never think the same. God built the woman to help man; stand beside him; love him; and help with his needs. Women have this twisted. She believes she needs. God did not say or create her for that reason.

> *Then the LORD God said, "It is not good for the man to be alone. I will make a helper who is right for him"(Gen 2:18 GW).*

It is so unnecessary for women to play games at all. She should understand who she is, and reason for her creation. She is man's gift. God built her to complement her husband. She is to complete him. If a man wants her as a complement, so be it. If not, it is nonsense for her to waste her time and talent. A man's approach ought to be with respect, considering she might be God's potential gift. If not, leave her alone. She is God's gift to the man who finds her to marry.

> *When a man finds a wife, he finds something good. It shows that the Lord is pleased with him (Prov18:22NCV).*

God created woman as an intelligent and articulate human being. She can detect a man's trustworthiness. God gave her special insight and the ability to sense what she often does not see. When she ponders, she can decide what she ought to do, or not do. Problems occur when women abandon the insight God granted them, and let their emotions control their decisions.

Persuasions

Women often influence other women to act according to their own behavior. Instead of girlfriends using an intelligent persuasive argument, counsel often arises from feelings. Interestingly, young or old, who experienced sex, enjoys rousing the one who has kept herself. After influencing the innocent to do the same, the innocent gives herself away. The girls pry their ears wide open to hear all the sorted details of her first intimate experience. It is all in fun, and she receives their applause to continue her sexual behavior.

Women today still choose to preserve their virginity until marriage. It may be an outdated idea for some, but many have chosen to keep themselves until marriage. Society's influence contradicts this assertion. So-called friends meddle in affairs, instead of befriending the choice to protect a friend's wholesomeness.

Women, who are not strong enough, collapse under the pressure, and stray into the arms of some jerk with no true affection or intent. He breaks and enters. However, through the influential urging of others, she permitted the robbery.

Unknown to her peers she struggles with humiliation, but smiles as if she is ok. Acting against her own desires, she hides her shame. She feels no pride in what she did. Although, her friends feel good about opening what she should have kept closed. Now along with them, she joins the ranks of the sexually self-exploited. Yet she cannot lift her hands to applaud herself.

Women Back in the Day

I can still remember conversations with mature women many, many years ago who believed in God. I can also recall the remarks of women who did not know God. The women who did not believe in God volunteered sexual information. I mean they said whatever they felt. They were not ashamed at all. They thought it was hilarious. They would detail everything, without asking you whether you wanted to know or not. You would stand there with your eyes popped out of your head and your mouth wide open.

Somehow, they spontaneously weaved sex into the conversation. Before you knew it, you were in a sex orientation class you never scheduled. These women told you what to do, and how to do it. What cream, potions, and lotions to use. They promoted your sexual promiscuity. These women, held nothing back in telling you how to perform, or detailing how a man performed on them. Needless to say, 'they were experienced.'

On the other hand, women who were in relationship with God taught you something different. They taught you about respecting yourself, preserving your dignity. They taught you not to fall for smooth talk, and to keep your legs closed. These women helped you understand your passions; how they awaken; why you needed to guard them, and release them to the husband who deserves you.

They understood a woman's hunger for love, but helped you understand how to tame your crave. They spoke from their wisdom and personal experience. They knew about life and the pitfalls that captivate women. They purposed to help you if you chose to listen. No one was overbearing, there was no need to be, these women could see right through you. They taught caution and safety. Most of all, they taught you to love yourself.

We know some men believe sex with several women give them bragging rights. A man can be a "hoe" as well as a woman. Society chooses not to regard men as such. Their promiscuous behavior reflects their manhood. Nevertheless, it is what it is. An apple is an apple. A pear a pear, and a "hoe" a "hoe," whether male or female. If sexual acts mirror each other, the actors are one in the same. Society uplifts men while devaluing women. When each commits the same acts, the descriptions of the acts do not differ.

Many women may not publicly boast. She may not verbally proclaim her sexual encounters, but her behavior announces them. What society is beginning to call the norm is not building, but rather, battering women's self-esteem. Intelligent as some may be. It is hard to hold your head up high when you dishonor yourself.

Be careful, society's progression is another's digression. Humiliating self is not normal, nor is the belief all is well when you do. Progressive ideologist will not think it humiliating, but rather, forward thinking. When forming new ideas, the forerunners attempt to convert convictions with new and improved mindsets contrary to God's. They would not term it self-humiliation, because one should consider the more open minded and progressive ideal for lifestyles nowadays.

Think about it; deliberate dishonor. If one dishonors self, and believes one does well, the thinking of that person is morally unprincipled. It reminds me of a scripture in Romans about reprobates.

Since they didn't bother to acknowledge God, God quit bothering them and let them run loose. And then all hell broke loose: rampant evil, grabbing and grasping, vicious backstabbing. They made life hell on earth with their envy, wanton killing, bickering, and cheating. Look at them: mean-spirited, venomous, fork-tongued God-bashers. Bullies, swaggerers, insufferable windbags! They keep inventing new ways of wrecking lives. They ditch their parents when they get in the way. Stupid, slimy, cruel, cold-blooded. And it's not as if they don't know better. They know perfectly well they're spitting in God's face. And they don't care—worse, they hand out prizes to those who do the worst things best! (Romans 1:28-32 MSG).

Women feel pressure to participate in sexual conduct prematurely. So, Why Did You Give up the Koochie and Now You Mad remains a valid point of reference. The question requires an answer. The answer has nothing to do with madness associated with anger. However, madness related to sadness and sickness of soul after yielding everything.

Do not get me wrong! Sex is one of the best gifts God created on the planet besides food. Old-fashioned as it may sound, God created sexual intercourse for enjoyment between husband and wife. You notice I did not say *for* the husband. A wife needs as much fulfillment as he. God did not create the wife as the husband's sex toy. He must remember he is her toy as well, if both choose to look at each other as such. Learn each other's want, satisfy them, and have fun doing it.

A husband should satisfy his wife's sexual needs. And a wife should satisfy her husband's sexual needs.

The wife's body does not belong only to her. It also belongs to her husband. In the same way, the husband's body does not belong only to him. It also belongs to his wife.

*You shouldn't stop giving yourselves to each other except when you both **agree** to do so. And that should be only to give yourselves time to pray for a while. Then you should come together again. In that way, Satan will not tempt you when you can't control yourselves* (1st Corinthians 7:3-5 NIRV).

Self Respect

Today, young women as well as the mature have lost self-respect. We have the bobcat and cougar targeting the same two-legged thing. What happened to embracing the idea of self-respect with women? Time and new ideologies loosened their embrace.

Oh no, you can scream and kick all you want. I am not out of touch. Because truth always remains, present, up to date, and current. It matters not whether people change their mind or ideas over time. Truth remains valid no matter how you slice it or dice it. Women's conduct, behavior, and thoughts have changed to reflect society, but not God's ideas about women. Society offers nothing in terms of answers for the brokenhearted who adopted new ideas.

An expression of freedom for women permeates throughout society. Liberation for women is wonderful. However, to liberate self from morals and standards invites shameful situations into your life. To continue in such conduct you must literally convince yourself to despise your shame.

There was a time not long ago, when women wanted the respect of men. They still do, but women adapting to the attitudes of men does not warrant it. You cannot act like a man, and expect respect as a woman. It is, as men acting like women, and expecting the respect and honor of a man. It is not going to happen.

Some say, "These are the old rules, anchored in past precept for our parents and grandparents; they are not for us today." Today's ideas influence women to do what she feels. If it feels good, have fun. The new idea suggests a woman be a tramp! With life evolving and women desiring to be equal to men, it has caused an extreme shift in behavior.

Men have been disrespecting themselves secretly as well as openly for years in their many indiscretions. Many women act out the same dysfunction, mirroring the attitudes of men. Progressive ideas challenge both young and old to toss their bodies from man to man without any regard or value for their secret possession. Both the young and the mature are promiscuous.

Freedom of Expression

My son received a phone call from a young woman one evening. He explained he was spending time with his family. He told her, he would talk to her on the following day. Well, about fifteen minutes later, to his surprise, the doorbell rang. She stood at the door asking to see him. Obviously, tomorrow could not wait.

The next morning, I asked him about their conversation. I wanted to know what was so pressing that she could not wait until the following day. Besides, I timed their conversation, which lasted a couple hours. Actually, that evening, I was curious, but decided to ask him in the morning.

We sat down in the nook for breakfast, I asked, "What did she want?" He said, "She didn't want anything. We weren't talking about anything." I said, "Oh, you were talking about something. The two of you talked for two hours. So what were you talking about?"

Hesitantly, he said, "She was just telling me that one of her girlfriends likes me, and if her girlfriend does not want to have sex with me, she would." I said, "Repeat that." He repeated it. "Ok, so her girlfriend likes you, but if her girlfriend does not want to have sex with you, she said, 'she will? What else did you talk about?'" He said, "We talked about some other stuff too."

The young girl and my son were the same age, fifteen years old at the time. I must be honest. What he said caught me off guard. I expected to hear something else, like, "She wanted to go to the movies." This young lady just met my son. She walked by our home with a group of girls. He was standing outside in the front yard. They stopped to talk, and told him they were visiting for the summer. After their giggles and laughs, they exchanged cell phone numbers and continued walking. Two days later, one of them rang the doorbell.

Now my son thought this was cute. By no means did I think it was charming at all. A young lady offering to spread her wings with a guy she does not know. He sat there and popped his collar, literally. She disfigured his mind. He thought that was awesome, a girl offering sex, if her girlfriend would not give him any. He could not see past what she said, nor consider, the consequences of both their actions.

However, I found it necessary to help him put life back into perspective and defend his future. He needed to understand the twist and the bait of the koochie trap. I had to explain a few things to him.

"If she will have sex with you and she doesn't even know you, she is acting like a "floozy." I am not talking about the kind you use to manicure a yard. She disregarded what you said, because she had something she thought more important. She came to your home after you told her you were spending time with your family. She thought it so important to inform you that her girlfriend likes you. That is not all. She said, 'she will have sex with you if her girlfriend does not want to.' She behaves like a "sexually toxic" teen. You think that this is something cute, well it is not.

Let this be lesson number one. This example is what you need to steer away from and avoid. You have goals and a future, a life full of unlimited possibilities. Do you want someone in your life for the rest of your life that you never intended? If she became pregnant, just think, for the rest of your life she will be there somewhere. Let us not talk about Sexually Transmitted Diseases (STD's); if she can serve it up to you like that, she has probably sliced the pie in several sections before you. You are probably going to get the scraps.

It is not to say she is a bad girl; she is just a sexually free and very careless one. Be careful of what you think is cute, because this is not. In one moment, a situation you think is cute, can and will change the rest of your life forever. I am certain you do not want to live a life full of regret. One bad choice is all you need for a lifetime of unwanted consequences. Think with your mind, and not with what is in your pants. You better consider what could happen before you do it."

Honesty

I am blatant and honest when I speak with my family, children, and friends. I am diligent in my attempt to help them to understand the consequences of an action. The result is their decision. Nevertheless, I try to explain the potential cost. Some listen, some to their regret have not.

Not everyone in society developed a sexual crave to satisfy his or her own flesh. There are young and mature women who still want to preserve themselves for someone who will respect and honor them. I still believe there are a number of women who disagree with societies progressive ideas. These women refuse to agree with the status quo. They uphold their value, and keep an uncompromising attitude of self-respect for themselves.

If a woman thinks of herself in this way, she simple agrees with the truth of God in her. However, if women embrace Gods' idea, societal ideas shun her thoughts as old and outdated. What ideals are better? Concepts that build you and make you better, or break you and make you worst. Who has a better conscious for your welfare than God does? If women embraced Gods' thoughts and exercised them, she can never go wrong.

Women ought never to encourage other women to let men screw them. Why have we dealt so unjustly, when we know a woman's emotional attachment? She must become harsh and cruel to strip away her nature, and become unfeeling. Without feeling and emotions, she can act like an animal; lie down; get up; and go on with her day. Do not feel or think; just swap body fluids, all is well.

God expects better for his daughters. Until a woman understands God's expectations for her, she will never live in His reality. She is not a sex object; her value is more than just for sexual pleasure. She is a human being, a person, a woman, whose passion runs deep. Because of the depth of her love, she easily bruises. I do not care how tough she is, under her hard core she is what God made...sweet and tender!

So many women hurt and are distraught. Women are moving from men hurting them to hurting themselves based on perception and a change in ideas. There are more broken and bruised women today than I have ever seen. The young woman is hurting; the mature woman is discontented. Hurt women trying to tell hurt women how to move through life unhealed. Women are pissed off, heartbroken, and live life as a shattered soul.

When women search to know the truth about what God said, and understand His idea of woman, wife and marriage. She will understand God's intentions and she will never think about herself the same. She will not allow a man to treat her any way he chooses. She will know God's declaration of how a man and husband should treat her. She will raise her standards to God's model of excellence. If, no one is around to meet those standards, she will wait for God to send someone to discover her. Instead of her looking in all the wrong places, and sending self through unnecessary madness.

Final Thoughts to Parents

Fathers and Mothers raising children are a challenge, but you cannot give up or quit. Press to invest in your daughters and teach them how to be young women, despite society's ideas for your children. Teach young women how to stand up and against unhealthy concepts that bring despair and shame into their life.

Please teach her the value of her treasure, instead of handing her a pack of condoms. She must learn the difference between what the world screams aloud, and the value God stamped on her life. Teach her how to possess herself. When those who think different, chatter a condescending word or use a belittling tone against her higher standards; she will not buckle under the weight of someone else's words. We are to teach our children with kindness and gentleness, not using words that hinder the course of their lives.

Parents, don't come down too hard on your children, or you'll crush their spirits (Colossians 3:21 Amplified Bible).

By perpetual faultfinding "children" are [athumosin] 'disheartened,' seeing the parents so hard to please. A broken-down spirit is fatal to youth (James, Fausset, and Brown).

They must know as little girls God's idea and love for them. The care, treatment, and consideration He declares for them. They need His solid foundation to stand on, grow, and become a healthy minded woman. Teach your daughters about the person in the woman. Teach your sons about the person in the man, so the woman receives the treatment God intended.

Women, who are brokenhearted, and downtrodden, run to the One who will heal and restore your heart. Run to the One who will build you up again. Run to the One who loves you more than anyone else. Take your heart and run to God. He will teach you the truth about you. He will teach you about true love, your creation, and the adoration He wants you to receive. He will teach you about the love affair He designed between husband and wife. He will teach you. Ask God, for what you need, "In the name of Jesus." He will not disappoint you.

Chapter Nine

Calculated Entrapment

S exy, let us place it on a silver platter and serve it to all who desire its intrigue. Let us market it on the world's stage. Let us fan its flames, let the embers travel across the globe and become the thing desired. Let us create images for ourselves and be enthralled by the flicker we create.

The world has developed its own calculated ways and methods to satisfy its pleasures. Listening to the world will turn you its way. Once its thrill for you vanishes, the world will vomit you out. You will look to find a remnant of your original person, if you can remember who that was. Those who knew you before the world turned you, will look, and not find you either.

Sexy, sexy, sexy, these words scream aloud to the citizens of the world. Have a bit of sexual prowess in your human character. What does that mean? Include sexual attraction or sexual attractiveness in your appearance. Please the eye with sexual appeal, evoke, and stimulate the beholder. Provoke the sexual senses in the opposite sex.

Today another term for sexy is *eye candy.* "Eye candy implies the subject is eye-catching in a superficial fashion by adding an element of sexuality. A sexual element can be an attraction influenced by a physical attribute." The visible attribute may be the way a person ambulates. Maybe it is the sound of someone's voice. Perhaps, the way a person smells or their smile. -Wikipedia

Sexy can be anything, influencing or affecting a person's sexual or erotic interest. Each person decides within him or herself, what is sexually attractive. Some sexual attractions become addictive. If a person abandons caution, one little peek of an image can turn a person upside down in a moment.

"*Addictive behavior* is any activity, substance, object, or behavior that has become the major focus of a person's life, excluding other activities. These addictive behaviors have begun to harm the individual or others physically, mentally, or socially." -Wikipedia

It is a recurring compulsion by an individual to engage in some specific behavior. Despite harmful consequences, as viewed by the user himself to his individual health, mental state, or social life. Many such processes within this concept are not harmful or deviant by themselves, but become harmful when they result in negative consequences. Frequently discussed examples include gambling, sex, eating, and internet usage.

"*Pornography addiction*" defined, by those who argue that it exists, is a dependence upon pornography characterized by obsessive viewing, reading, and thinking about pornography and sexual themes to the detriment of other areas of life. -Wikipedia

A host of sexual attractions continues to lead men to sexual addictions. We can lay the blame for most dysfunctions on human nature or the mortal man. If we choose, we can point fingers at those who we believe are at fault, or who we think are to blame. Dynamic influences and sexual persuasions amuse, incite, and play with the senses of men.

For many they congest the psychological and emotional reservoirs with ideas that effect reason. So why do we dance with the enemy and play with things that are unhealthy for our soul and well-being? Do we believe we can taste, yet not be touched by the thing we sample? Scripture asks,

> *"Can a man scoop fire into his lap without his clothes being burned?"* (Proverbs 6:27 NIV)

The answer seems simple. Yes. Interestingly, many scoop heaps of fire in their lap, believing a burn will not occur. They throw common sense out the window only to return with the question, "How in the bleep did I let this happen to me? So why do people touch things they know they should not? What makes the temptation attractive? We learn from Scripture that one tempts his own desires. The Scripture teaches,

> *"Each one is tempted when he is carried away and enticed by his own lust. Then when lust has conceived, it gives birth to sin; and when sin is accomplished, it brings forth death.* (James 1:14-15 NASB)

Lust, passions, and desires stir when provoked. This is one reason I say molestation of the mind is a cruel enemy to any man's soul, male or female. What germinates in the mind, forms roots, and dominates one's thinking. The more the mind entertains, greater is the thought fortified. Sound judgment takes a step to the side and leaks out the back of the mind, like a slowly dripping faucet.

As thoughts are entertained they become more pronounced, and one's original mind distorts and twists into its obsession. The subject's intelligence provides no defense against such vices. The only defense is to guard one's mind from destructive influences. Influences addict the mind, as well as one's passions to their hurt. If the seed remains rooted, one finds self-moving toward the contaminated thought. Scripture teaches, "You must *'be careful how you think; your life is shaped by your thoughts'*" (Prov 4:23 Todays English Version).

> *'Guard thine heart; but: before all that one has to guard, guard it as the most precious of possessions committed to thy trust. The heart is the instrument of the thinking, willing, perceiving life of the spirit; it is the seat of the knowledge of self, of the knowledge of God, of the knowledge of our relation to God, and also of the law of God impressed on our moral nature; it is the workshop of our individual spiritual and ethical form of life brought about by self- activity-the life in its higher and in its lower sense goes out from it, and receives from it the impulse of the direction which it takes."*
> - Keil and Delizsch Commentary

Mind Molesters

Most people when they think of the word "molestation" they think of someone acting in a perverted way against a child, and this understanding is true. However, a disguised form of mind molestation exists. No one calls it molestation, because it hides behind a door named beauty; but it is just that...molestation of the mind.

Molesting a man's mind, troubling, bothering, or harassing it; is practiced for the explicit purpose of arousing and stimulating settled passions through the eye gate. The eye considers its subject, taps on the mind, as if to knock on a door waiting for an invitation to enter. When the door opens, it gains access. Passions ignite for the thing that crossed and entered the eye.

For this specific reason, arranged images manipulate men's minds. The one, who promotes the image, captivates the one who lusts after it. Mind molesters, entangle, and bind the molested, by igniting a desire for the images presented.

An old art form provides a supply, by creating a demand for its particular kind of product. A man can create a desire in the mind or heart of another man: by photograph, video, or telephone conversations.

He can then supply his customer's sensual desire; and create a perpetual consumer; moreover, a habitual client. How clever is the method to entrap, entangle, and bind one by his own lust. The art of developing a strategy to initiate a crave using one's own passions for profit and financial gain.

What a profound form of seduction. Some men discern the craft and choose willingly to comply. While other pompous and senseless men hold fast to the lure. Either way both are still caught in the "mind molesters" net.

In one form of pornography, women dress the pages of magazines as articles of beauty. Many men choose to believe that this is just a natural attraction. They elect to believe there is nothing wrong with what occurs to them when they flip through the pages, drooling at women in the raw. Those who delight in such say, "It is a normal indulgence for a man's appetite." Many men would beg to differ. They know where perversion can and have led them.

For those men delivered from pornography they advise that this is not a healthy appetite for any man. However, every man must make his own decisions. Still, men who choose to dabble in the lifestyle would probably not share this part of their life with their mother, sister, or wife. They know it is neither good nor healthy, but they do it despite what they know.

Artwork

Mind flirtation is an aged old concept, tried and proven to work. Satan did it with Eve in the garden. She looked at something God had forbidden her to entreat. However, through Satan's conversation, he molested her mind with a thought of possibilities, and stimulated her appetite.

Now the serpent was more crafty than any of the wild animals the LORD God had made. He said to the woman, "Did God really say, 'You must not eat from any tree in the garden'?"

² The woman said to the serpent, "We may eat fruit from the trees in the garden, ³ but God did say, 'You must not eat fruit from the tree that is in the middle of the garden, and you must not touch it, or you will die.'"

"You will not certainly die," the serpent said to the woman. "For God knows that when you eat from it your eyes will be opened, and you will be like God, knowing good and evil."

When the woman saw that the fruit of the tree was good for food and pleasing to the eye, and also desirable for gaining wisdom, she took some and ate it. She also gave some to her husband, who was with her, and he ate it. Then the eyes of both of them were opened, and they realized they were naked; so they sewed fig leaves together and made coverings for themselves (Genisis 3:1-8 NIV).

She allowed another's voice to manipulate her gaze on something she never considered. When she looked, she saw it provided a source of satisfaction and was good for food. She saw the same tree and passed by it for however long she lived in the Garden. Until one day, a conversation stimulated her mind to look and desire what she had not thought of.

She knew God's word; she repeated exactly what He said. Nevertheless, through an interchange of thoughts, deception entered her mind, and she allowed it to overrule God's Word. It cost both her and her husband's life. Spiritually they died.

The same thing occurs today. Voices, whether by words or deeds, introduce ideas not previously thought of, and manipulate the mind to not only notice, but to also yearn. Suggesting something deadly and hoping for its acceptance. It caused the spiritual deaths of God's first living souls, and man still flirts with killing his spirit.

Flirtations' use is to attract the sexual attention of the intended target, to encourage romance or sexual relations. Flirting is the foundation on which seduction builds it strength. Seduction is a bit more serious; it is a calculated process used deliberately to entice another to engage in sexual relations. Flirtations' best friend is time. Time prepares the cocoon for the target, and unknown to the individual a hole waits with an open mouth for the fall.

There are many influences specifically tailored to lure and ensnare the simple minded. This would be understandable if perhaps true. Simple-minded men are not solely the victims the artists seduce. Brilliant minds easily bend when overtaken by desire. To their discredit, they have lost wife, house, children, respect, and a lot of money.

Forbidden Women

In the book of Proverbs, Solomon teaches his son to watch for women with flattering lips, and cautions him about women with flirting eyes who bat their lashes (Proverbs 6:20-25). Solomon is the wisest man of all time. God endowed him with wisdom and the ability to judge a matter in excellence. In all his wisdom, it did not save him from the folly of his fleshly desires. God specifically warned him to keep away from forbidden women.

Although Solomon knew God's instruction, his voracious appetite for foreign women turned his eyes and heart away from God. Foreign women were a delicious desire, and his attraction was deeply rooted in all of them.

His own personal experience gave him a vantage point by which to teach his son about the art of seduction. Solomon was educated in its trickery firsthand. This prohibited experience would also be the catalyst for his removal as king. Solomon betrayed God when he became unfaithful; he stopped serving the Lord with his whole heart.

Solomon rendered his heart to pleasures for himself with his foreign wives. He built high places for all of them. In his later years, they seduced him to follow their foreign gods. Solomon's disobedience cost him his kingdom (1st Kings 11; 1-43). However, the wisdom, he gained through his observations, he strongly warns his son against.

My son, pay attention to my words. Treasure my commands that are within you. Obey my commands so that you may live. Follow my teachings just as you protect the pupil of your eye. Tie them on your fingers. Write them on the tablet of your heart. Say to wisdom, "You are my sister." Give the name "my relative" to understanding in order to guard yourself from an adulterous woman, from a loose woman with her smooth talk.

From a window in my house I looked through my screen. I was looking at gullible people when I saw a young man without much sense among youths. He was crossing a street near her corner and walking toward her house, in the twilight, in the evening, in the dark hours of the night. A woman with an ulterior motive meets him. She is dressed as a prostitute. She is loud and rebellious. Her feet will not stay at home. One moment she is out on the street, the next she is at the curb, on the prowl at every corner.

She grabs him and kisses him and brazenly says to him, "I have some sacrificial meat. Today I kept my vows. That's why I came to meet you. Eagerly, I looked for you, and I've found you. I've made my bed, with colored sheets of Egyptian linen. I've sprinkled my bed with myrrh, aloes, and cinnamon. Come, let's drink our fill of love until morning. Let's enjoy making love, because my husband's not home. He has gone on a long trip. He took lots of money with him. He won't be home for a couple of weeks.

"With all her seductive charms, she persuades him. With her smooth lips, she makes him give in. He immediately follows her like a steer on its way to be slaughtered, like a ram hobbling into captivity until an arrow pierces his heart, like a bird darting into a trap. He does not realize that it will cost him his life.

Now, sons, listen to me. Pay attention to the words from my mouth. Do not let your heart be turned to her ways. Do not wander onto her paths, because she has brought down many victims, and she has killed all too many. Her home is the way to hell and leads to the darkest vaults of death (Proverbs 7:1-27 GW).

Seduction

When you develop a concept or method of sexual persuasion, can you call it seduction? If you use what you understand to coerce, lure or entice a person, or society to take part in improper conduct; is it seduction? If a person creates schemes to tap into another's conscious, to crack into their subconscious to intentionally stir desires that lead to lustful passions, is that seduction? If a man understands another man's sexual weakness, manipulates what is vulnerable, is that a form of seduction? Yes it is.

I am not referring to man as the male gender; I am talking about women as well. Who is responsible for seduction, men, or women? Women allow the use of their bodies for display. Men in turn use this to target the weaknesses of men. The images compel men to look at a little cleavage exposed here, a little thigh showing there. The cover of magazines, movies, videos and the internet inundates society with explicit sexual graphic images.

"Traditionally pornography was created for male viewers. However, the numbers of women viewing pornography is increasing substantially. What use to be a degrading sport solely for the pleasures of men, women find pleasure in as well. Feminist movements have arisen to fight on opposite sides of this argument. They are the "sex positive movement" and the "anti pornography movement."

The *sex-positive movement* is an ideology, which promotes and embraces open sexuality with few limits beyond an emphasis on safe sex and the importance of informed consent. Sex positivity is "an attitude towards human sexuality that regards all consensual sexual activities as fundamentally healthy and pleasurable, and encourages sexual pleasure and experimentation."

The sex-positive movement is a social and philosophical movement that advocates these attitudes. "The sex-positive movement advocates sex education and safer sex as part of its campaign." The movement makes no moral distinctions among types of sexual activities, regarding these choices as matters of personal preference. http://en.wikipedia.org/wiki/Sex-positive

On the other hand, the term *anti-pornography movement* describes those who argue that pornography has a variety of harmful effects to the user, such as sexual desensitization, dehumanization, sexual dysfunction, and inability to maintain healthy sexual relationships. And to others, in the form of encouragement of abuses such as human trafficking, pedophilia, and sexual exploitation.

People involved in the anti-pornography movement include religious groups, feminist, ex-porn stars, psychologist, and individuals who feel that pornography plays a major role in the breakdown of marriages and relationships. http://en.wikipedia.org/wiki/Anti-pornography

Everyone has the option to choose, "What shall be your influence?" Your influences will build you, or kill you. It can build you into the person you hope to become. Influence can also kill you, and invite you to become what ideologies, or philosophical beliefs suggests. You best decide how you choose to govern your life, by Godly principles, or philosophical arguments that will eventually send you into a living hell.

Pornography, a License to Kill

The pornographic industry is a multi-billion-dollar business that employs women to solicit men. More than seventy percent of male internet users between the ages of 18-34 view internet pornography sites on a monthly basis. More than seventy percent, that is a large number of men, and these statistics apply only to this age group.

The methods are more sophisticated, but the concept remains solid. Instead of using women in brothels to coerce men, they spread across pages, whether through magazines or the internet. The technique offers a simpler access that allows men to discreetly peek, in their home, on their computers, at work, or on their cell phones. They believe no one sees, but God sees everything. When you hide your behavior that is the first red flag, indicating something is wrong.

Men influence women to believe their beauty should display itself to the world. Be bold and shameless. "Everyone should see how beautiful you are. Beauty should not be hidden, nor is it anything a woman ought to be ashamed of." Open your legs and anything else we can photograph, show, tell and let us sell to the world." You have simple-minded men, and you have simple-minded women. The world influences both souls to fall into the same trap.

The same-old game is constructed with different players. Without using women, no game exists. However, women have joined the cause and agreed with the men who use them for their profit! A couple of influencing words and a few dollars and they strip naked. Some might not consider this a method of pimping. Nevertheless, women can be pimped on the page, or she can be pimped on the street. Either way men use women to seduce other men today. A problem exists when the thought processes of people are so manipulated they can no longer discern the difference. They begin to agree and believe likewise. Like calf going to a slaughter, led astray.

It is a legal method of the new day pimp; the strategy of selling sex for a billion dollars. They are raking in money as sexual addictions of men and women increase. Women on the street sells the sexual experience, while the women draped across the pages sells the fantasy. Both consent to men doing ungodly things because of pornography.

Oh! I forgot some women have come to agree with, and bought into the fallacy that she should not keep her beauty to herself. She ought not to be ashamed to let the whole world see her legs spread wide open, closed, or see her bent over. Then there are the others whose feet willingly carry them into the arena, joining the ranks of those who fuel the appetites of indiscretion. Women solicit themselves for center page coverage as they agree with the "beauty phenomenon."

Women have lured men for ages. They used themselves to seduce men from the beginning. Yet, immeasurable is the way men have used women to entice and arouse the sensuality of men. Who has the largest craving for pornography...men. Who are the people at the forefront of these vast markets...men.

One could say, 'men have become provocatively skilled in derailing the passions of men for profit?' I say, "Yes." Men cause the feet of men to stumble, using women as their bait. Interesting, is it not? What is more interesting, both allow it. The women who love to incite; the men who enjoy the arousal; and the industry that manipulates both while taking the money to the bank.

Man found a way to betray men, by understanding how to awaken and incite a lascivious appetite; and feed its lust. They learned how to stir, provoke, satisfy, and entangle men for their financial security. Sadly, most men believe it is the woman's fault; had she not removed her clothing, and taken photographs, or made that video, he would not suffer such temptation.

The last statement is partially true; a woman exposing her nakedness perpetuates negative and addictive sexual behaviors. However, let us take it a step further; had another man not seen the opportunity to use man's lower impulses against him, it would not be a billion-dollar industry either. Men procure women to assist in their plight to snare men into sexual perversion.

> *Blessed (happy, to be envied) is the man who is patient under trial and stands up under temptation, for when he has stood the test and been approved, he will receive [the victor's] crown of life which God has promised to those who love Him.*
>
> *[13] Let no one say when he is tempted, I am tempted from God; for God is incapable of being tempted by [what is] evil and He Himself tempts no one.*
>
> *[14] But every person is tempted when he is drawn away, enticed and baited by his own evil desire (lust, passions).*
>
> *[15] Then the evil desire, when it has conceived, gives birth to sin, and sin, when it is fully matured, brings forth death.*
>
> *[16] Do not be misled, my beloved brethren (James 1:12-16 AMP).*

A Porn Star's Story

I must say not all women involved in the pornographic industry is there because they chose the life. I read a revealing statement written by Linda Boreman (Lovelace). She claimed in her autobiography that violence, rape, forced prostitution, and private pornography plagued her marriage. She wrote:

> *"When in response to his suggestions I let him know I would not become involved in prostitution in any way and told him I intended to leave, [Traynor] beat me up physically and the constant mental abuse began. I literally became a prisoner, I was not allowed out of his sight, not even to use the bathroom, where he watched me through a hole in the door. He slept on top of me at night, he listened to my telephone calls with a .45 automatic eight shot pointed at me. I was beaten physically and suffered mental abuse each and every day thereafter. He undermined my ties with other people and forced me to marry him on advice from his lawyer. My initiation into prostitution was a gang rape by five men, arranged by Mr. Traynor. It was the turning point in my life. He threatened to shoot me with the pistol if I didn't go through with it. I had never experienced anal sex before and it ripped me apart. They treated me like an inflatable plastic doll, picking me up and moving me here and there. They spread my legs this way and that, shoving their things at me and into me, they were playing musical chairs with parts of my body. I have never been so frightened and disgraced and humiliated in my life. I felt like garbage. I engaged in sex acts for pornography against my will to avoid being killed...The lives of my family were threatened."* –Wikipedia (Lovelace)

By now reader, are you wondering why this topic is here? Too many Christian men and women struggle with sexual lust. We have seen the evidence of it more and more over the last several years in the Christian community. It has damaged some of the best of us. Men as well as women must understand the methods and tactics undermining their soul.

I thought her story, however sad, interesting, and worth mentioning. She was a young woman forced into prostitution and pornography. She testified before the 1986 Attorney General's Commission on Pornography in New York City, stating, "When you see the movie *Deep Throat*, you are watching me being raped; It is a crime that movie is still showing; there was a gun to my head the entire time."

Why are these acts against women condoned? Condoned because, Christian dollars view pornographic material, instead of using those dollars to fight against its abuses. These women are someone's daughters, sisters, and mothers. Where is the coalition of men who stand against such mindsets? Where is the coalition of men to serve and protect the safety of women in spite the opposition? Where are those who stand up against exploitation, instead of remaining silent about a woman's indecency?

The Scripture teaches the faithful not to conform to the ideologies of the world. However, let your mind be and stay renewed by the "Word of God." The renewal process is a daily endeavor to not only read, but also remember. Throughout your day, you will converse with numerous people; not everybody will be talking to you about God. You are the faithful; you are responsible to remember to walk in the Word. The Spirit of God enables us to do so. If your soul does not have roots in God's Word, conversations with worldly people will mess you up.

> *I appeal to you therefore, brethren, and beg of you in view of [all] the mercies of God, to make a decisive dedication of your bodies [presenting all your members and faculties] as a living sacrifice, holy (devoted, consecrated) and well pleasing to God, which is your reasonable (rational, intelligent) service and spiritual worship.*

² Do not be conformed to this world (this age), [fashioned after and adapted to its external, superficial customs], but be transformed (changed) by the [entire] renewal of your mind [by its new ideals and its new attitude], so that you may prove [for yourselves] what is the good and acceptable and perfect will of God, even the thing which is good and acceptable and perfect [in His sight for you](AMP Romans 12;1-2).

Perversion is a hook in the depraved mind. Beauty is the bait sitting on the hook to lure the catch. Lust hooks the catch and snatches it into the net. Men find themselves caught and snared by women through men. The industry enlarges its nets for a greater fall and catch. The nets stay open as the bait dangles to gather more souls. Soul trapping, and why not, wealth rides on those who slip into a bottomless trap.

Addiction

Some men are ashamed of pornography's addictive grasp. Many men regret what became of them after their first look. They regret taking that peek of a naked girl in a magazine. The first sight was amazing. Until magazine after magazine, an obsession began brewing. Passion took a turn from normal, to searching for more of the girl on the page.

Men found themselves prisoners to their own thirst. After satisfying their eyes, it drove them to want to see more. All addictions are progressive. It may initially start with a peek in a magazine, then to full-length videos, then the real experience with a hooker, and wherever else perversion takes them.

Not all men who find themselves in this situation choose to remain in it. However, they do not know how to become free from the lust that wars against their soul. The addiction is deeply rooted, emotionally and psychologically. However, God by His Spirit is able to uproot every stronghold in a person's soul. Hallelujah! Praise to the One and only true God.

I spoke with a man who was candid about his addiction to pornography. He said, "The reason it is so addictive is because of the intimacy you acquire with pornography. It is an intimate relationship; you develop with self, and very difficult to break. You are addicted to a self-seeking, and self-gratifying obsession. It is hard to climb out of the trap of sensual impulses, because the images are always in your mind. It becomes something you constantly think about, and look forward to."

I Like What I see

Men say they are visual creatures. Are not women as well? I would have to agree with the first thought being more prominent than the second is. Women glance and admire men, but I have yet to see a woman stumble down a staircase because a man's appearance hypnotized her. However, I must add, a woman recently confessed this happened to her.

I have seen men stumble down stairs, run into the back of vehicles, and walk into other people. I have seen men fixated on women, paralyzed and stuck. Luckily, none of them injured themselves in these instances. I witnessed men peek out the corner of their eye before a woman escaped their view. I watched men scratch their head to turn around to catch that final peep.

Eve's appearance took Adam breath away. When Eve crossed Adam's sight, the Scripture explains that he was astonished with surprise. You must understand what this means; Adam was smitten; he was overtaken! The words, "*this is now* (lit., *this time*) *bone of my bones*," etc., are expressive of joyous astonishment at the suitable helpmate (Keil & Delitzsch Commentary).

Adam named all the animals, and saw nothing compatible for him. However, when God presented Eve, Adam filled with a force of emotion and overwhelming shock. Man, yet remains astonished at the sight of a woman, recognizing and being overjoyed that she is a suitable companion.

There is one little catch; God created that joy, astonishment, amazement, and surprise in man for his *own* wife. This joy is not for Sarah, Suzie, or Jody. His heart fills with joy for his wife. He finds joy knowing, she is as he; flesh of his flesh and bone of his bone. Scripture teaches that a man and his wife become one flesh. A man cannot be one flesh with several women; though he may try, he can only be one with his wife.

Well, you might say, Adam did not have all the choices. No, he did not! However, what God created in him was for his wife. God did not change his mind over time; a man's excitement is still for the wife he finds. Granted he needs to look, observe and investigate in order to find his helpmate, but that does not infer searching for her at the drop of his zipper. He need not pull the zipper down, to investigate.

Men have the choice to *find* a wife. Not choose excuses for participating in unprecedented sexual relationships that he attributes to being male. A man cannot become one flesh with several companions. He can become soul tied, which is more than a physical bond. However, these sexual connections need to be broken. He only becomes one flesh with his wife. When he finds he forsakes all others and commits to leave and cleave.

> *Therefore, a man shall leave* (loosen, relinquish, forsake) *his father and his mother and shall become united and cleave* (to impinge, cling or adhere to) *to his wife, and they shall become one flesh* (AMP Genesis 2:24).

Do not allow the world to define your identity. They will applaud you to do whatever you feel, and influence you to be who they say you should. It will be everything that is contrary to God's idea. Guard your most prized possession…your heart; all of your decisions flow from its seat. Watch and pray that the nets men have set do not catch and trap you. By some chance, if they do, fall at the feet of God, and ask Him for deliverance. He will provide the grace and mercy, to repair your soul.

God has a solution in the most difficult of situations. When we think we have wronged ourselves to the point of no return; God has a remedy. Sometimes He grants immediate freedom or deliverance, and in some instances, He processes you out of it. He uses time to eliminate attachments; removing one reason and cause at a time. God will give the strength and grace to overcome the most challenging set of circumstances, if *you* want change. We tend to forget to remember that our battles are spiritual, not natural.

> *3 For though we live in the world, we do not wage war as the world does. 4 The weapons we fight with are not the weapons of the world. On the contrary, they have divine power to demolish strongholds. 5 We demolish arguments and every pretension that sets itself up against the knowledge of God, and we take captive every thought to make it obedient to Christ. 2ⁿᵈ Corinthians (NIV) 10:3-5*

Chapter Ten

Influence –

The Power of the Koochie

In the Garden of Eden, most people who read about Adam and Eve's affairs do not equate her handing the forbidden fruit to Adam as influence. She knew no sin, how could she influence him to do wrong. Yet she disobeyed God's command. The moment she decided to disagree with God's authority she began her decent into sin. This profound matter needs our close attention.

Eve conversed with the serpent, the serpent challenged her truth, and she considered what she heard; dishonored God's instruction; picked the forbidden fruit; and then ate. After all these sequential events, her eyes did not open. At the point of her conscious decision, she became insubordinate. She thought it before she ever committed the act. She disobeyed God long before she ever bit the fruit. Yet, nothing in that particular moment happened. It took Adam's bite for them to fall.

If Eve did not hand the fruit to Adam, what would the consequences have been? What would have occurred? We can only speculate. If Adam refused, and reiterated God's command, what might he have intercepted? We can only wonder. Is it not an interesting and compelling thought? What would God have done, if Adam did not take what his wife offered? Would he have saved his wife and self, because of his obedience? Only God knows.

God brought Eve to Adam as his wife. Literally, Eve was bone of Adam's bone and flesh of his flesh. They truly were one; God built her from his flesh and bone. Because of their union, when Adam bit they both spiritually died. In Adam's disobedience, he failed to cover himself and his wife, and brought high treason against God. Adam knew what God said, but he listened to his wife's influential voice. I wonder what she said. Whatever it was, his agreement cost them their life, as they knew it.

Some might argue Eve did not influence Adam. Well, why did he respond with a yes instead of a no? Her influence carried no deceitful intentions. She and Adam were one. Their response with one another was without question. She knew nothing about such antics of deception. She did not give Adam the forbidden fruit with the intent to deceive, but rather, to share in her disobedience.

Adam was not deceived, because he knew, as well as Eve what God commanded. She trusted another's words, because all she knew was trust. A lie, what was that? Deceit, she did not understand its methods. Had she known listening and responding to another's words besides God's would cost her life, she would never have listened.

Eve had no idea an act of disobedience would trust her out of her home, and put her soul at odds with God. If she knew, she would have rejected the serpent's words. Why should she not trust, if she had never been acquainted with deceit? What was the meaning of death, when void in knowledge of its sting. However, she possessed personal information regarding Her Creator's Word. Obedience is better than sacrifice. You never know what the penalty of disobedience requires.

Now Adam could have rejected her offer, but he accepted it. He too knew God's command. What is the power women possess that cause men to rise, as well as fall, when they know better? What is this attribute or skill passed from Eve to women since the beginning? It is the power of influence. How potent is the power of a woman's influence today?

Eve knew what God had commanded both of them. Somewhere in her mind, between the time she conversed with the devil, picked the fruit, and ate; she decided to influence her husband to share in her disobedience. She wanted the possibility of what the fruit rendered. Her desire for what was possible silenced God's Word, and led to her into a disobedience act. She had no idea or concept of God's consequences.

This is fascinating. What Lucifer desired originally, to be like the most high (Isaiah 14:12-15), he deceived Eve through her passions. He manipulated her want. Eve's will turned from God to her desire. Her conversion came while listening to what she heard and looking at what she saw. Satan knew that if he could manipulate her desires he would destroy their life, and their intimacy with God. Jesus watched Satan thrust from heaven for desiring after the same thing.

> *Jesus said to them, "I watched Satan fall from heaven like lightning (Luke 10:18 GW).*

> *How you have fallen from heaven,*
> *O star of the morning, son of the dawn!*
> *You have been cut down to the earth,*
> *You who have weakened the nations!*
> *¹³ "But you said in your heart,*
> *'I will ascend to heaven;*
> *I will raise my throne above the stars of God,*
> *And I will sit on the mount of assembly*
> *In the recesses of the north.*

¹⁴ 'I will ascend above the heights of the clouds;
I will make myself like the Most High.'
¹⁵ "Nevertheless you will be thrust down to Sheol,
To the recesses of the pit (Isaiah 14:12-15 NASB).

Scripture teaches: *"every person is tempted when he is drawn away, enticed and baited by his own evil desire (lust, passions). Then the evil desire, when it has conceived, gives birth to sin, and sin, when it is fully matured, brings forth death* James 1:14-15AMP). Scripture gives no period from sin's conception in Eve to their death. However long, or short, we know sin is a process.

Eve's influence persuaded Adam to pay attention to her words. Although she knew, exactly what God commanded, as she repeated, and reminded the devil of God's Word. Satan deceived Eve with the possibility of what the fruit potentially had the power to offer. Satan stirred in Eve a desire to want, not to want anything, but to want what would kill her. Satan evoked a passion in Eve to want something she should never have put to her mouth. Desire and passions are deceiving. The knowledge of good and evil she and Adam acquired, cost them their spiritual lives.

Influential Power

God gave women something incredible, the power of persuasion. God bestowed this gift upon every woman. When Eve transgressed, God did not take her influence. She kept it. Influence was not the sin; disobedience to God's commandment was the error. Her desire to satisfy self above God's Word proved to be the transgression. God said, "Do not," and she and Adam decided, "We will." Knowing God's Word, together, they agreed to sin.

God has intrinsically placed in every woman this awesome attribute. She can use it for good or evil. A woman ought not to use her hereditary ability gifted by God for seduction, enticement, or deception. Its purpose is to influence husband, brothers, sisters, and children to obey God.

Remember woman was built to contribute to the fulfillment of man's need. God created woman to further man's efforts and support his purpose, not destroy him. A Godly wife can influence her husband to conduct himself according to God's Word. However, an irreverent wife can persuade her husband to do as she delights, neglecting the Godly use of her gift to suit his best interest.

A wife decides how she will choose to administer her influence. She can opt to persuade her husband toward those things that are admirable: good; honest; honorable; respectful; beneficial; truthful, and excellent. Alternatively, she can decide to influence her husband into: deceit; indecency; dishonesty; disloyalty; deception; greed; callousness; immorality; perversion and false pride. The worst always seems to produce more than the best.

God placed an enormous power in the hands of women to use as a tool and asset. When its purpose is misunderstood, so is its use. So many women have used their influence for personal satisfaction. We know, as well as witnessed the power of influence women utilize on men. Often on men who are not their husbands. She exercises her power to fulfill her self-seeking gratification at the expense of another woman's hurt. This is madness.

When God created the man and the woman, He created them as husband and wife. God ordained the first marriage when He brought Eve to the man He built her for. God gave His first daughter to her husband, and sanctioned their union. Marriage is a holy union created by God that deserves the upmost honor and respect.

> *Let marriage be held in honor (esteemed worthy, precious, of great price, and especially dear) in all things. And thus let the marriage bed be undefiled (kept undishonored); for God will judge and punish the unchaste [all guilty of sexual vice] and adulterous.* (Hebrews 13:4 AMP).

Some might suggest that the events that occurred many millenniums ago in the Garden, have no bearing on our lives today, except the sweat of a man's brow and the labor pains of a woman. We still feel the effects of the penalty of Adam and Eve's sin. A direct correlation exists between the Adam of yesterday and the decedents of Adam today.

Yesterday's Adam did not contend with Eve. He did not debate or argue the truth; he just submitted to what she said and ate what she offered. There was no fight, no resistance. He did not question her offer. Although, he knew God told him not to eat, he did it anyway.

So how did this happen? Did Adam remove the forbidden fruit from Eve's hand, or did she put it to his mouth? For now, we do not know. Yet, what is sure is this; upon God questioning Adam, he pointed Eve out as the culprit who influenced his disobedience. Adam response to God when questioned was, "The woman made me do it God. It was the woman you gave me."

God asked, "Who told you that you were naked? Did you eat fruit from the tree I commanded you not to eat from?" The man answered, "That woman, the one you gave me, gave me some fruit from the tree, and I ate it" (Genesis 3:11-12 GW)

The Scripture reads as though Adam not only blamed Eve, but God as well by inferring, "it was because of the woman *you* gave me." Adam said, "I did not have anything to do with it. That woman you brought to me, she did it. It was just You and me God, just You and me. You are the One who gave me that woman. It is not my fault God; it was You and me, until You brought that woman to me. She made me disobey You God. She did it!" You get the point.

What is the different between Adam's influences and man's influence today? How often do men blame women after their fall? How many men do not fall, but dive into a woman's offer? No resistance: no fight; just, a voluntary submission to what she suggested; eyes wide open; lost in the moment without understanding, or neglecting to consider the consequences.

That is not to say that all men entangle easily by a woman's influence. Many men understand the attraction God placed within him for his counterpart. He also understands how to defend and preserve himself for his wife. An admirable quality some have not acquired. Nonetheless, numerous men allow women to sabotage their homes. They fall to the wayside instead of standing to protect and defend self, as well as wife and family from divisive female schemes.

Cheating Cheaters

A woman should not covet another woman's relationship, or marriage. Too often, the jealousies of women long for the affection and care given to a wife by her husband. They stand adjacent watching and wanting. Admiration and appreciation of a husband's affectionate love toward his wife is acceptable. Nothing is wrong in that.

The problem arises when she wants for the same affection, and her want is for the husband she admires. In this hope she grossly errors. Instead of waiting until God sends a prepared man her way, she would rather opt to trade places with the wife she also adores. Admiration trades places with jealousy. Soon jealousy fuels her craving lust, and she conjures ways to work her influence. Deception is a cold calculating work.

She becomes infatuated with a thought, and makes inappropriate use of her gift. Her intent is to draw his attention from his wife toward herself. This too is madness, and a sick condition of the soul. Women orchestrate such acts, and men great and small collapse at their feet. Instead of pointing the finger at self, he points toward the woman. Both are equally guilty, she for choreographing the trap, and he for committing himself to the fall.

We have witnessed, if not been a victim of the "hoochie koochie" mama. That is what I call this type of female. We have seen them work their campaigns successfully. They replace men's wives with themselves. No regard for anyone else; consumed with their own selfishness.

Cheaters are captivated by the intrigue, and neither husband nor koochie mama stop long enough to consider the lives they will shatter. The only consolation either of them offer is, "I am sorry, I never meant to hurt you," "Hogwash." If a person never means to hurt you, they will deny themselves of everything potentially damaging to you, to protect your heart. That is a tall order; nevertheless, there are men and women who faithfully defend their spouses every day, with a heart of honor.

A woman's premeditated thoughts induce charges against her own conscious. A husband's first thought after she captures his attention, he knows is wrong. Instead of casting down imaginations, he lifts them up, and entertains them, but so does she. She should have seized her initial thoughts and discarded them. But no, she played with them until her ideas crept into her passions. Both birthed desires for something they each should have aborted.

> *The world is unprincipled. It's dog-eat-dog out there! The world doesn't fight fair. But we don't live or fight our battles that way—never have and never will. The tools of our trade aren't for marketing or manipulation, but they are for demolishing that entire massively corrupt culture. We use our powerful God-tools for smashing warped philosophies, tearing down barriers erected against the truth of God, fitting every loose thought and emotion and impulse into the structure of life shaped by Christ. Our tools are ready at hand for clearing the ground of every obstruction and building lives of obedience into maturity* (2nd Corinthians 10:3-5 MSG).

I know it is a little difficult to walk in the Spirit when someone is in your face tempting your weaknesses. Nevertheless, you better; your life depends on it. You will look around dumbfounded and confused, asking, "How in the hell did I let myself get in this situation." By the time, you ask that question, it is already too late, not to mention the aftermath that follows.

> *Now those who belong to Christ Jesus have crucified the flesh with its passions and desires.* ²⁵ *Since we live by the Spirit, we must also follow the Spirit.* (Galatians 5:24-25 HCSB)

The above verse does not imply that you kill or crucify passions or desire as though you are lifeless. God placed these affections within you. We crucify the sinful nature we lived in without the Spirit. Since we have a new Spirit, we put that old nature to death. We follow in a new way of life consistent with the Spirit's nature. We no longer yield to; *"idolatry and witchcraft; hatred, discord, jealousy, fits of rage, selfish ambition, dissensions, factions* ²¹ *and envy; drunkenness, orgies, and the like"* (Galatians 5:20-21 NIV).

Choices come with results or consequences. The outcome depends on what choices we make. Both male and females make awful choices displaying irreverent behavior. Just like women, some men will see a woman that belongs to another man, and want that man's wife. You can disagree, but that is an evil blow to the core of the human heart.

Abandoning Conscious

For cheaters to cheat each must abandon their guilty conscious, lay it aside, and proceed in satisfying what drives them. They call this an accident or mistake. It is not an accident. This is an accident. A woman fell, a man tripped, and his penis just happened to fall inside her vagina. Now that is an accident where one could say, "I am sorry, this was a terrible mistake." If this did not happen, it is deliberate. The 'I am sorry' story really does not apply. On the other hand, maybe, it was a mistake. It was a mistake to make reservations, drive to the Resort, obtain the key, strip butt naked, and commit adultery. Ok, big premeditated mistake, I am moving on.

God has declared all to honor marriage, and what He has joined; let no man put asunder (Heb 13:4 & Matthew 19:6). This is an evil that women do to women; unyoke a husband from his wife, and it needs to cease. A woman should never use her gift of influence to overthrow another woman's husband. We know this happens, and often, but it should not! She ought to utilize her gift on her *own* husband and not target it for random seduction.

Men must be conscious not to fall prey to the subtle influences either. Women are good; trust me, very well equipped indeed. Husbands guard your heart and mind, and protect yourself from what flows from you. An unprotected *heart* and *mind* adds vulnerability to the lower impulses of human nature. Never leave either unprotected. Man's nakedness exposes him to the evil nature of his own desire he draws to himself. Scripture calls these senseless men (Proverbs 7:7).

God has instructed His children to guard their heart. Place a fortress: a garrison around it to protect it, and defend it from allowing evil to enter; but also from allowing evil to exit from it. From the seat of the heart is where the matters of life are determined. Keep your hearts from any tainting, so with sound judgment you may rightly conclude a matter.

Scripture teaches us that every thought that exalts itself against the knowledge of God, we cast them down, and bring it into the obedience of Christ (2nd Corinthians 10:5). Through the wisdom, and counsel of God's Word, we protect; defend; guard; and cover our heart. When we fail to submit to the Word of God's power, we find ourselves powerless and overthrown by the will of our own flesh. If we do not submit to the "Spirit" we will submit to the desires that work against us (Galatians 5:16).

There is so much that has not changed, although thousands of years have come and gone. This is not new; this is the old state of fallen man. If we are clueless to our fallen nature and the tactics, the devil articulates against us. We will continue to fall with our eyes wide open. We must operate from our spiritual conscious, if not; the lower impulses of our nature will overtake us.

I hope men grasp an idea of woman's influence. I hope he realizes how some women use it against them. Especially, those women who are not their wives bidding for their attention. I hope this raises awareness in men about their impulses, and their need to protect themselves, as well as their family.

Influence itself is not bad. What is bad is what fuels it. If the fuel is corrupt so are the influential tendencies. A perverse nature works against all of us. So now, with perversion fueling influence, the devil brewed a recipe to ruin souls. He ruins through man's own want, desires, lust, craves and passions. Men beware; influential women are equipped to satisfy all those cravings, if you allow it. Stand and do not fall for the influences that evoke and call for your lower impulses to arise. God is able to keep you.

I have a great admiration for God's image. I find this intriguing because men are intellectuals. Nevertheless, when it comes to their passion, influences sideswipe them. We know men influence women as well. We all discuss this issue. However, we never openly expose the seductress. Yes, men seduce; but a woman's cunningness when used with her influence far outweighs a man's by a long shot. Men believe they are seduces. However, women seduce men into believing he seduced her. She gets what she wants; while he believes it was his idea.

Be alert. God created you to lead with sober mindedness, and passions intact. It does not mean exhibiting hardness, or cruelty; showing unkindness, lack of passion or love. Rather, live life in the knowledge of God's Word; Christ died for this.

I talk so much about the beauty, magnificence, and wonder of a woman, and her understanding God's idea of who she is. Men you should understand as well, how beautiful, wonderful, and awesomely you were made by God. You are fabulous. Understand God's mind for you as well.

I hope that men are able to recognize the entanglements set by women. I hope women acknowledge and consider the influence gifted by God and the reason for the gift. I hope women understand their responsibility of influence, to bring out the best of a person and not the worst.

God's Grace

The personal guilt and shame attributed to this kind of behavior is painful. We find ourselves guilty. Our deeds shame us, for allowing our flesh to consent, to what we knew was wrong in the first place. Overall, God is here to forgive us of our faults, and heal us of our guilt and shame.

Sometimes forgiveness is more difficult when we need to forgive ourselves. However, we must forgive self for our mess. Thank God for His grace. Not only does He forgive and heal, but He also grants to us second chances. We need to thank Him for giving us an opportunity to do what is right. Be grateful He allows us to correct our choices and live.

In The Garden

Did you understand what transpired in the Garden? This is the reason we received grace, not because we deserved it, but because we are helpless without God's mercy. Our passions sabotage us the same way they sabotaged Eve in the garden. We see something; we hear something, and step over God's Word to satisfy our want. Our desires, our will, our passions are corrupted. It does not take much to become defenseless to immorality. A glance, a wink, a smile, and our soul contaminates with perversion.

Oh! Blessed it be the God of Glory. There is hope for our predicament, a way to fight against the passion that war against us in God through Christ Jesus. Through Christ Jesus, the soul regenerates. When you accept Jesus Christ as Lord and Savior, God's Spirit resides in you empowering you to live contrary to your self-indulgent sexual appetite, as well as any other sinful nature. As you were dead in your inabilities, the Spirit enables you to live in a new and free way. The Spirit of God is all-powerful. God is able to make you stand in the midst of temptation. Choose to stand with Him; His Spirit will keep you from falling.

Chapter Eleven

When A Man Finds...

oday, women chase men much more aggressively than before. They seek to find themselves a mate. A woman used to wait for a man to approach her. That is no longer the case. A man was the aggressor in the pursuit of a woman to wife. With the changing wind of time, it blew out the idea of patience for...and blew in the idea...of chasing after. The mentality of women toward men, and men toward women changed drastically.

Women have become aggressive pursuers. They pursue not necessarily to wed a husband, but just to get a man. She now wills to bust the sweat off her brow in exchange for hubby to stay at home. For her, that is ok, because at least she has a man. She exhausts herself as she leads, instead of standing beside. She willingly displaces herself outside of God's divine arrangement, and easily frustrates when he fails to meet her expectations.

Let me clarify something before we continue. If a woman temporarily supports her husband, due to some unforeseen circumstances, she does well. If a woman chooses to employ herself in the workforce, that is fine. However, she ought not to become indignant, because she employed herself. Support your husband. You and he are a team; do not ever forget who you are.

Now some women who employ themselves in the workforce refuse to support their husbands financially. This is ridiculous. The ridiculous part is that she has it within her means to help him, and would rather watch him suffer financially. I am not talking about a man who has never contributed. That is another story within itself (why do women even go that route?). I am talking about men, husbands who have been there, taken care, loved, and stood by a woman's side. Now he struggles with a financial difficulty. Write the check, pull out the money, and help him!

This is troubling; some women would rather let their husbands suffer. However, they will go purchase clothing and whatever else, which counts for nothing, while disregarding his financial need. Financially, she is capable of assisting her husband. Nevertheless, she refuses to help him through his difficulty. Women always talk about what their husbands need to do for them. What about what a woman needs to do for her husband? Especially when he proved himself as a true man, and husband as well. What happened in the heart of his good thing? What happened to compassion and consideration?

Now some women will pony-up. In other words, girlfriend will do what is necessary to ensure matters stay intact. She will have his back while helping him rise to his feet again. If he finds it difficult to return to the work force, it never becomes an issue. They will modify, recalculate, and formulate a new plan, because they understand love, unity, and oneness. This is teamwork.

Care for him, and help him rise back upon his feet. God created you with the components to know what to say; know how to deliver it, and support his confidence in him. When he knows you have not lost your confidence, it helps him sustain his. Faith and belief ignites a man's self-assurance to envision he can rise above the storm. Do what is necessary and let no one convince you otherwise. Work your teamwork.

Now listen up, if he is an able-bodied man and capable of providing, but too lazy. You know, one of those males who lie on the couch, watching TV all day. One who hangs out with his lazy friends? A male who waits until the woman comes home from work, and ask for money. "Do you want a man that bad? " Are you that lonely? Then choose loneliness over someone who will not get up and provide." Why accept a male who refuses to become God's definition of a man. Why accept less than what God prepared you to receive, why? Let us continue where I paused, regarding God's divine arrangement.

God placed hunting and pursuing in man, not in woman. I know society tells you it is a new day, and a new dawn for women. Society will tell you anything, and everything contrary to God idea for your life. Indeed, this may be society's reality, but it is not God's. People change their mind over time, yet God's mind remains stable. Today both men and women see relations much differently. Nevertheless, God's order remains intact.

We change, thinking we have evolved. In many instances, we regress from a divine order to a self-seeking state of existence. Anytime, we step out of God's arrangement; it may appear, we progress, but we digress rapidly. We fall from a higher order of living. God's principles still apply; His Word is eternal and never outdated. Therefore, it remains fitting for a man to find...

Scripture teaches that, "*A man who finds a wife finds a good thing and obtains favor from the Lord* (Proverbs 18:22 HCSB).

Understanding the Definition of Man

Who is a man? Let us investigate this question and find its answer. Let us stroll back through time into the Garden. In here, we find where man began. When God created *man,* He created them male and female, and made them in His image (Genesis 1:27 HCSB). God first made man before He built woman. Before the female, man stood alone. Man was not lonely, just alone without a suitable companion.

Before God introduced Adam to his wife, He introduced Adam to a J.O.B. Work was the first assignment Adam received from God. He gave Adam responsibilities. His responsibilities consisted of the care; maintenance; and preservation of the Garden. Adam learned to work and take care of his home. God planted the Garden, placed Adam in the middle, and gave him charge of paradise. Adam received responsibility, authority, and dominion.

A responsible man learns how to become accountable. Accountability is a process developed through experience. If a man marries without learning responsibility when the pressures come to support his family, it may destabilize him. Because he has not learned, what responsibility means.

His marriage will become his learning process. Unfortunately, that process can become overwhelming. He can learn with the assistance of his wife if she loves with patient and kindness. However, that may take some time. Responsibility teaches through experience. It develops understanding and wisdom to know what and how to do something.

God gave husbands serious responsibilities. For this reason, it is essential for a wife to honor and respect her husband. He is the family head; the responsible for the religious life of his family, he is priest and prophet of his home. He is the house-band that connects his whole family; he is protector, provider, and defender of his household.

A husband loves, takes care of and oversees the lives of his family. He ensures he provides the best for them. He is mature, responsible, sensible, intelligent, wise, prudent, cautious, and careful. He is mature psychologically and emotionally, and his disposition reflects such character. This by no means is the sum, just notable characteristics. A husband is awesome! Not that a single man is not, the focus here is on the husband.

Finding the Rarity of a Thing Obtained

As we can see, the husband has a list of weighty responsibilities. He is the leader, the one who points the way for his family. In order for him to direct, means he has a family; which means he found a good thing.

This word *find* is very interesting, because the Scripture teaches that when a man finds, he found something *good*. However, because of the cultural climate, women initiate the chase to find themselves a "thang." This conduct opposes the order of God. God did not create man for the woman, but woman for the man. Let us keep it correct.

I am aware that we are living in a different culture, with different attitudes and mindsets. Nevertheless, God did not tell the woman to search for a man to become the complement of him. God created woman for man's finding. Instead, she is out with a search party looking for him.

In order for him to find her, he needs to look. This might sound antiquated, an outdated method of pursuit, but it is not. Some beg to differ and disregard God's Word. However, time has no bearing on what God established.

Let us be clear about seeking. In man's search, he seeks for a woman to wife. The purpose of his search is to find his complement, not a woman to carry out his sexual desires. His complement not only completes him, but she delights in gratifying his needs.

The word *find* implies the rarity of the thing searched for and obtained. He should look for her with careful consideration and circumspection. Not merely to satisfy a compulsory act of the flesh's desire.

He should understand what he wants long before he begins his search. A man, who seeks a wife with circumspection and supplication, finds a good thing. He finds his rare and precious jewel complementing himself.

A *good thing*, what is the meaning of this expression? It means grace: union, peace, order, power, strength, and plenty. However, it also speaks of a good wife's duty, her virtue, and being prudent. Her duty is to be morally obligated. Her virtue reflects the expression of God's will: moral excellence, goodness, and worth. Her prudence knows how to use discretion, avoiding embarrassment, and being careful and sensible

A good wife says the Talmud, "is a good gift; she shall be given to the man who feareth God."

The word *"wife"* is a name of honor. A man, who finds such a woman, deserves the honor associated with the name. Wife is a prestigious word, worthy of the woman who accepts its title. A woman who desires marriage should prepare herself, not for the title alone, but also for a wife's responsibility. She should examine herself, to understand her own capabilities, attributes, and disciplines.

A woman must know her identify, if not, someone else will define who she is. She needs to remain true to herself, before she walks down the aisle to say; "I do!" Just because a man asks a woman to marry, does not mean she should marry that man. Not every man and woman is suitable for each other in marriage. Just as he must consider and inspect, so must she!

The scripture reads, "He who finds a wife finds a good thing; and obtains favor with the Lord. (Proverbs 18:22 NASB)

The word "*favor*" has several different meanings. The Septuagint renders favor as cheerfulness and joyousness. It also means good will, acceptance, and benefits that flow from cheerfulness and joyousness as well. Favor represents the position a husband enjoys before God, and the favorable disposition God holds toward him. In addition, the husband recognizes God's favor, acknowledging nothing occurs because of his own efforts. Favor also renders as *grace* as well, meaning, undeserved consideration.

> *Matthew Henry's commentary reads, "A good wife is a great blessing to man. God is to be acknowledged in it with thankfulness; it is a token of his favour, and a happy pledge of further favours; it is a sign that God delights in a man to do him good and has mercy in store for him; for this, therefore, God must be sought unto."*

A wife is indeed a good find. A good to her husband not inherited nor deserved. Every man who stands before God and becomes one flesh with his "good thing" can accredit God to the highest blessings in his life. Her disposition is not simply pleasing to him, but he also favors her above any other. His desire and passion are for her and towards her intently. He finds the utmost pleasure and joy in his wife.

> *In a true marriage, a man's wife is his best friend. The fellowship of soul makes the union more than a mere contract of external relationship. Now, this fellowship is greatly needed for solace amid the caress of life, and strength to face its difficulties. The wife can give it to her husband, and the husband to the wife, as no persons in the outer circle of social relationship can hope to offer it.*
>
> *A woman is degraded when she is treated as a toy of idle hours, to amuse in the drawing-room, but not to take or share in the serious concerns of life. No true woman would desire so idle a position. The wife who understands the*

Christian calling will aim at ministering to her husband in all ways of helpfulness that are within her power, but chiefly in helping his higher life; and the duty of the husband towards the wife will be similar. The wife is not the counterpart of the husband, but the compliment! Therefore, is not the part of women to imitate men, nor is inferiority to be assigned to women because they differ from men. The rich full, perfect human life is attained by the blending of differences. ~The Pulpit Commentary

Husband and wife ought to become best friends. I would go as far to say, "Best friends before marriage." Who besides your spouse can you stand naked before and lay vulnerable? Not naked as unclothed, but nakedly standing with a disrobed heart. Allowing your best friend the privilege to see, what no one else gets an opportunity to behold. You share everything with your husband or wife, and tell anything without fear and anxiety? God designed husband and wife to share the most intimate bonds on the earth.

What are the secrets of marital blessings, and the process of its manifestation? Confidence must be mutual between a husband and wife if the relationship is to be a lasting one. Both must have the utmost respect for each other. They must equally care to do their best for one another, and forfeit selfishness. They should season their words with love and kindness, and take care as to what they say, and how they speak their words.

Cruelty or degradation on either part is a fatal poison to the union of marriage. Selfishness is another toxin that will destroy marriage by pulling it apart. Be careful to consider one another above self. The husband and wife must learn how to delightfully give themselves to the other, suffer with one another, and endure through the rough time, as well as the joyous. Each should earnestly desire to satisfy the needs of the spouse.

Happiness may be wreaked on so many hidden rocks that it is not safe to venture on to the unknown sea without the assurance that God is guiding the voyage. ~ The Pulpit Commentary

Chapter Twelve

Husband

*W*e understand a little about what the word *"husband"* means from the prior chapter. The word itself actually means *house-band*. A house-band means; one who bands his house together. He is one who fastens, joins, unites, connects, holds, and keeps his family unified. He supports, sustains, and provides sustenance to preserve them. Husband means giver, nurturer, and provider. He is the authoritative figure in his house, not as a dictator, but as one who encircles his family in wisdom through love.

A house-band serves his family as one who pours himself out. He nurtures them, in order that they might realize their own greatness. He encourages his house to reach toward their potential. He makes the most of his family, by unifying, and not by scattering. He sits in a place of great responsibility. His position and title require honor and respect.

He is the primary responsible to take the required measures to provide leadership for his household. Just as Christ did what was necessary to lead the church. He inquires of the Lord, how to govern his family. Scripture's truth binds him securely to his duties, role, and responsibilities. Through his leadership and authority, his wife rests safely. He builds her up with honor, respect, and love. He is a prototype of Christ and examples the love affair between Christ and His church.

The relationship between husband and wife should reflect the romance between Christ and His bride, the Church. What is Christ's relationship? He is in love with His body. Christ cherishes, defends, protects, provides, nourishes, treasures, nurtures, sustains, loves and supports her. Christ is not rude, cruel, harsh, unforgiving, condemning, demeaning, and self-seeking.

Scripture teaches husbands to dwell with their wives according to knowledge. He ought not to dwell with her according to his passions or lusts. He ought to dwell with an intelligent observation as a wise and prudent man. He should be a sensible man who understands their relations and his duty to his wife. Thereby, allowing his well-informed observation and understanding to master his actions toward her, and govern his own steps accordingly.

He should recognize what Scripture teaches in relation to her being more fragile. The wife is more delicate than he. In some translations, it reads that she is the "weaker vessel." It does not imply that she is less intelligent or her mind operates at a declined or lower mental state. She is not mentally incompetent, inferior, or pathetic. She most certainly is not!

The wife is weaker in the sense of physical strength. A man's bodily strength rivals hers. God made her gentler, sensitive, affectionate, delicate, and fragile. She is more apt to subject to infirmities, because of her body's fragile state. Her physical strength and stamina are not equal to that of a man. Since she lacks these particular features, she exhausts and fatigues more easily.

The husband ought to recognize her frailties and sustain her lack giving due consideration to her weaknesses. She needs to dwell with him appreciated, and treated with special care and kindness. Furthermore, the husband is to render her honor and respect as well. Scripture asserts that she is worthy of esteem, as she shares equal inheritance in the "gift of life." The husband and the wife are heirs together; equally called to glory.

In the same way, a husband must live with his wife with the proper understanding that she is more delicate than he is. Treat her with respect, because she also will receive, together with you, God's gift of life. Do this so that nothing will interfere with your prayers. 1st Peter 3:7 (Good News Bible)

1. The particulars are, (1.) Cohabitation, which forbids unnecessary separation, and implies a communication of goods and persons one to another, with delight and concord. (2.) Dwelling with the wife according to knowledge; not according to lust, as brutes; nor according to passion, as devils; but according to knowledge, as wise and sober men, who know the word of God and their own duty. (3.) Giving honor to the wife - giving due respect to her, and maintaining her authority, protecting her person, supporting her credit, delighting in her conversation, affording her a handsome maintenance, and placing a due trust and confidence in her.

2. The reasons are, Because she is the weaker vessel by nature and constitution, and so ought to be defended: but then the wife is, in other and higher respects, equal to her husband; they are heirs together of the grace of life, of all the blessings of this life and another, and therefore should live peaceably and quietly one with another, and, if they do not, their prayers one with another and one for another will be hindered, so that often "you will not pray at all, or, if you do, you will *pray with a discomposed ruffled mind, and so without success." Learn, (1.) The weakness of the female sex is no just reason either for separation or contempt, but on the contrary, it is a reason for honour and respect: <u>Giving honour to the wife as unto the weaker vessel.</u> (2.) There is an honour due to all who are heirs of the grace of life. (3.) All married people should take care to behave themselves so lovingly and peaceably one to another that they may not by their broils hinders the success of their prayers. -Mathew Henry Commentary*

A husband's disposition should be regarding and not defiant. He should lead his wife away from danger, and not subject her to negative consequences. Nor position self to exhibit disdain towards her. It does not benefit him to conduct himself arrogantly or think he holds some level of superiority.

These behaviors are usually the evidence of a prideful man. Unreasonable pride abides in the bosom of foolish men void of wisdom. We know wherever pride abides; destruction follows closely behind. Usually, a prideful husband asserts unwarranted authority over his wife due to his insecurities hidden within him. They are insecurities perpetuated by his fears.

He must come to terms with his private lack of self-confidence. He must govern his concerns, to present himself upright before his wife. His desire to receive honor and respect are contingent upon them. A wife delights in her husband presenting himself well, whether at home or in public.

Submission

A wife's greatest gift to her husband is her honor and respect of him. He cannot force her to present him with her tribute. If he is not an honorable and respectable man, she cannot give what she does not possess. He cannot expect a return without any investment. The investment is his love, and his return is her honor.

Most husbands preoccupy themselves with the wife fulfilling her duty. Yet, he refuses to submit what God instructed him to surrender. A wife's response, submission, and agreement predicate upon her husband's love. His love ought to resemble Christ's love; the love Christ displayed for His church.

When Scripture teaches wives to submit, agree, and place themselves under their husband's leadership. It means just that... leadership. Scripture further teaches a wife's response should be as unto the Lord. Husbands, often forget this particular verse.

If the husband's resemblance contradicts Jesus, he probably will not receive the response he wants. How can she respond as unto the Lord, if his demeanor does not resemble the Lord? She cannot appropriately respond to what does not remind her of her Lord and Savior.

Although, without a husband loving his wife as Christ loves His people, she may commit to acting out physical wifely functions, without ever esteeming him in her sight. A woman can perform wifely duties without holding her husband in honor and respect. However, if he wants her honor and respect, he should learn she would respond to what God instructed him to surrender. A woman responds, submits, and yields, to a husband that cherishes, loves, cares, and sets his interest aside to address her *needs*.

Empty Vessels

If not love, why yield? She cannot agree, submit, respond, or place herself under anything less than love. A husband can try to force her, but willingly her heart will not respond. She will struggle and fight within herself to give honor she does not have. She cannot render what is non-existent. It is impossible.

God built a woman to receive nothing less than faithful love. She will submit, yield, and surrender to it. She will respond to loves leadership. She will agree to what is good, kind, loving, tender, and gentle. Her will does not fight against such things.

She delights in these beneficial qualities, which supports her soul's health. She will respond to her husband's love, as she would respond to the love of Christ. She will not fight against love. She will not quarrel with what is sweet and dear, she will agree with it.

Now, if her husband is unloving, she will battle a war within herself. Submission and honor will be her greatest struggle. A husband's love reciprocates honor and respect from his wife. She loves him because he loves her. (I am not talking about ingrates. Ingrates are women whose husbands cherish and desperately love them. However, they refuse to respond to his love. They are not a part of this equation!).

I have met wives who perform duties just like a job; they cook, clean, and care for their husband and children. However, they find no desire for him. They do not love, honor, or respect him. They exhibit the characteristics. However, they are void and empty; a shell of a woman; performing the duties of a wife.

Naked and honest women, who speak the truth, sometimes shock you by what they say. Some said, "Love, honor, and respect did not exist. They stayed to keep their home. Some said they stayed for their children and waited for them to mature. They said they lost their love because their husbands never gave his.

God created woman for man to complete him. However, He also built women as recipients of love. If the husband does not submit and surrender his love to his wife, the husband neglects filling her heart. Her heart beats empty, void of what God created her to receive. As long as her heart is vacant, her husband will never receive the level of honor and respect God created him to enjoy. Both, husband and wife when submitting to God receive what God placed within each to satisfy.

Is there a wife who does not want her husband to fall head over hills about her? What husband does not want the utmost honor and respect from his wife? No robbery exists where both husband and wife humbly submits to the other.

A husband can strip a wife's spirit by withholding his love from her. "So husbands do not destroy her passion and desire for you by withholding what belongs to her. You can make her, or break her up into little particles. If her thrill for you vanishes, it will take nothing less than a miracle from God to resuscitate what you starved. "Love fuels the appetite of its desire and fills the lungs with oxygen to live. Be the fuel of your wife's desire, and the oxygen she must have in order to breath."

Remember the Scripture in Genesis, where God told Eve her desire would be for her husband. Consider this, although God sentenced her to *crave* for her husband. That is not a permanent condition. Listen, based on the husband's actions, he can nurture and sustain her passion that God lit on fire. Alternatively, the husband can smother the blazing flame over time. The rise and fall of her flame depends on how he treats her.

God is not responsible for keeping her fire lit. That is contingent upon the husband's continuance to woo his wife unto him. He is the only one who can extinguish what God put in her for him, based on his disposition and attitude toward her.

God forbid, the husband and wife dissolve their union. If she becomes another man's wife, her desire rekindles for that husband. Now we know God does not agree with divorce; but in our disobedience, and hardness of heart, it happens. Now although the first husband blows out her flame, he did not eradicate her desire. It reignites and she responds to her new husband.

Wives understand and support your husband's in ways that show your support for Christ. 23 The husband provides leadership to his wife the way Christ does to his church, not by domineering but by cherishing. 24 so just as the church submits to Christ as he exercises such leadership, wives should likewise submit to their husbands. Ephesians 5: 22-24 (The Message Bible).

Husband and wives understand; a wife should not submit to what is against her conscience. Nor for that matter, submit to anything that her husband insists is detrimental to her safety or well-being. She is not to submit to what is morally destitute or illegal. Her obedience is to God first. She will stand and give an account for deeds performed in her own body. Her husband will not stand by her side speaking on her behalf, saying, "God, I told her to do it."

I remember attempting to take part in Women's fellowship. I thought I would participate for clarification and understanding of scriptural text relating to this particular subject. During a discussion, the women said, "You must obey whatever your husband tells you to do." Therefore, I asked, "What if your husband wants you to go somewhere you do not want." The response was, "You have to do what he says, and God will hold him accountable."

Therefore, I asked another question, "What if your husband wants to watch you have sex with another man?" Their response, "Your husband is responsible, and God will hold him accountable." I discontinued my attendance. I thought that was rather ignorant on their part.

For we must all appear and be revealed as we are before the judgment seat of Christ, so that each one may receive [his pay] according to what he has done in the body, whether good or evil [considering [a]what his purpose and motive have been, and what he has[b]achieved, been busy with, and given himself and his attention to accomplishing] (2nd Corinthians 5:10 AMP).

They believed whatever your husband told you to do; you just do it! Now, although Adam and Eve were husband and wife, both received different judgments. God judged them independently. Adam and Eve received judgments for their own sin. A husband has no dominion over his wife's conscience. She must do what is right before God.

A woman is responsible to God for her own actions, and must give God an account for them. She must stand before God alone and for what she has done in her own body, just as her husband must. He will not and cannot stand before God on her behalf. Each must stand before God separately, on their own accord.

Force and Violence

The husband should not malign the will of God concerning his wife's life, but support her in it. Not all men, but some believe women have no call of God. This is far from the truth. What God called a woman to do for His glory, a husband ought to support. This by no means gives a woman a right to disrespect and dishonor her husband. God created order, and that order reflects unity, not division. Husbands ought to understand God's call upon their wives and allow her the room to move in, and with God.

God positioned the husband as a leader, not commanding officer. He ought not command her, or force her to do anything. God gave her a will; along with her will, God also gave her choice. She decides whether she chooses to yield or not. He is not a dictator. He cannot force her submission. Nor threaten her with violence, or use physical aggression to beat her into submission. That is not the will of God, nor is it the conduct or position of a spiritual leader. The husband's conduct ought to reflect him as priest and prophet of his home.

Scripture teaches the husband to lead his wife in love. Love does not beat, but lovingly teach. If he beats her, are these the lessons she should learn? When he strikes her, can she do, likewise? If she is to follow his leadership, does she apply what he taught? What a devastating union. Who wants to live in a house full of contempt and hell? Who wants a marriage where both husband and wife beat each other?

Christ does not force or beat His body into submission. He loves His body in such a way that the body desires not to offend

Him. Christ lovingly instructs His body, to receive, in full, the benefits, for which He sacrificed Himself. Therefore, we who are Christians submit our will to His instruction to please His uncompromising love.

When we closely observe how He has so loved us. Because of his love, we desire to satisfy His heart with our response of obedience. When the wife finds herself cherished, respected, honored, acknowledged, and treated well, she desires to submit to love's sweet nectar. It is her desire to please her husband and respond to the love he demonstrates.

Non-Submissive Husbands

I have often witnessed husbands who quote Scripture eloquently regarding the wife's responsibility. They reference Eve's deception. On and on they go as though Scripture was a tool used to keep their wives restrained. Because of Eve's deception, and God creating Adam first they stand in defense of their superiority. I have yet to hear them elaborate about Adam's gullibility.

Satan tricked Eve by a lie. Adam complied with an offer. Some scholars suggest that Adam was there during Eve's conversation; he said and did nothing. While other scholars imply Eve was away from Adam conversing on her own. We may not know for certain, which is correct. Nevertheless, we know, Adam was the first recipient of God's Word. Adam, the first man, committed treason, and blamed his wife for his disobedience (Genesis 3:12).

Somehow, when discussing, husbands loving wives as Christ loved the church, it is not the number one topic for men. This subject matter is a rarity. Wives obey your husbands is a much more comfortable theme. They find the subject of her submission more compelling than their own.

Husbands oftentimes are forward in asserting, and or binding wives to Scripture. Interestingly, they loosen the ties for themselves. Their ties are so loose they release themselves of the responsibility to reflect Christ. Many husbands desire their wives to respond according to the "Word of God." Yet, they lack discipline in demonstrating Scriptural leadership. Neither do they respond appropriately to the dictates of God's Word pertaining to loving their wives as themselves. A husband wants his wife to obey him, without submitting himself to the obedience of God first.

Submission is an uncomfortable word for many husbands to embrace. However, submission is a word that a husband needs to understand. The word does not apply to his wife alone. Both husband and wife are to submit to one another (Ephesians 5:21). Submission is the act of yielding, and agreeing with one another.

When a husband yields his love, the wife submits her honor. She does not yield or submit honor, or respect because she must. She does because she wants to. She yields under the weight of love, as if in a drunken splendor. Her husband can virtually get whatever he wants when she is overtaken and intoxicated by his love.

When captivated, she desires to humble herself. A duty given by instruction becomes a natural yearning to satisfy. Why is this so? It is, because in love there is safety. It comforts and calms the rhythm of the heart. It renders peace and silence to the mind. It seeks to please. It promotes a harmonious environment. It reflects the interest of the loved. It ponders, considers, and contemplates for the good. It invests in its future. It is kind, appealing and evokes love to itself. It navigates through wisdom and sound reason to be beneficial. It is strong, yet sweet and tender. It is complete.

Love is patient and kind. Love is not jealous or boastful or proud [5] or rude. It does not demand its own way. It is not irritable, and it keeps no record of being wronged. [6] It does not rejoice about injustice but rejoices whenever the truth wins out. [7] Love never gives up, never loses faith, is always hopeful, and endures through every circumstance. [8] Prophecy and speaking in unknown languages[a] and special knowledge will become useless. But love will last forever! (1st Corinthians 13:4-8 NLT)

The husband is responsible as the leader to be the first responder, not the wife. His position is in the forefront and he leads by example. It is not the responsibility of the wife to assume his position as leader. Christ did not require His body to love Him or obey Him beforehand. He showed His love prior to receiving the obedience of the people for which He came and died.

> *However, God demonstrates His own love toward us, in that while we were yet sinners, Christ died for us.* (Romans 5:8 New American Standard Bible)

Do as I Say Do

Communication is a crucial component and a priceless commodity in marriage. Some of us are more effective talkers than others are and enjoy the exchange of words. A wife desires her husband to effectively convey his thoughts and desires, so she can develop a full understanding of who he is.

A husband who does not enjoy conversing with his wife will find this a challenge, if not outright irritating. When he considers a matter, and brings it forward, she questions his reasons. It should not frustrate him. Especially if she finds no basis for what he considers. If she questions, he has not dotted all his I's and crossed all his T's. There is something not complete, a component missing, or the timing is off.

Often, operating out of pride, he will want her to just "*do as I say do*." 'I am the husband, I have the final word, and this is what I am going to do!' Wives save husbands from numerous mistakes when they listen. When they do not they return with apologies.

"Now you can be the king of your castle, but what manner of king are you; dictator or a Lord? No one loves a dictator, because his rule is harsh and evil. However, one, who rules as Lord, draws love to himself by what is good, pleasant, and decent. Dictatorship oppresses every part of the human soul. The soul screams to free itself from oppression

Wives are not partners who become invalid and silent speakers. God gave her a voice and a mind to communicate on an intellectually level. Through communication, she has a right to express her thoughts, insight, and ideas. By doing so, she proposes what God created her to do, help form decisions.

A well-respected king, listens, considers what is best for those under his care. He receives love and honor, because of his consideration. Those under his authority benefit from his goodness toward them. His queen delights in strolling through the courts of their castle, seeking God's will for her husband, house and self.

God created her as a companion with whom her husband can receive counsel. She listens regarding all of his decisions as well as plans and strategies, and offers her godly guidance. She will assess the benefits against the consequences for the security of her family. If he honors her, he will seek her advice and wisdom, which will keep him out of harm's way. She will help him preserve the unity of their house by avoiding decisions he might regret.

When a husband disregards the wise counsel of his wife, usually, he finds himself in a situation. If prideful, she may never hear him apologize for discounting her counsel. If he is not full of pride, he will confide in her what occurred, and apologize for not regarding her advice.

An intelligent wife insist on knowing who, what, when and the why of it all. When the husband researches and gathers information, he can inform intellectually. She can comprehend what he considers more clearly. Furthermore, when she knows he invested time to evaluate his decision, she is more confident in his leadership.

If there is a decision, he wants to make that he has not thought out, she will not agree. She has no confidence in his decision. All the while, she listens with her ears hinged on every word. She is paying close attention to ensure she hears his covering and wisdom.

A wife who communicates her concerns to her husband is not attempting to stand against him. She is merely trying to understand him, as well as, him understanding her. Do you notice how a large majority of wives seem suspicious? One thing that wives have over husbands is the trickery in the Garden.

Eve realized the method of deceit, which cast her from her home. Deception taught her a valuable lesson. Eve passed down her enlightening experience to thousands of generations. Women stay on high alert watching for potential threats of deception. They are cautious with anyone's words, especially their husbands.

Deception is women's most hated enemy. She despises lies and deceit, and absolutely hates the practice of them. A husband, who desires his wife to trust him, should first invest the time communicating to her why she should. After the fact, it becomes trust by demonstration.

Blind trust belongs to God alone. God is the only one whose words are true; He cannot lie. Do not expect a woman to yield to blind trust. You must earn trust. Talk the talk; live in truth, and preserve her confidence in you.

In order for the wife to be secure in her husband's decisions, he must be an effective communicator. That means he must invest the time to explain and comfort her concerns with his words. Wives who have husbands, who do not communicate well, also have wives who live in uncertainty.

Wives are capable of understanding, but often, husbands do not invest the time to explain their position. Wives, not only become unsure, but also frustrated. When husbands neglect to entreat wives with their words, it translates as insignificant, and invalidates what she needs to comprehend, making her feel unimportant. What appeared as a sweet woman when first married; now appears as a tyrant, enraged all the time; battling emotions of insignificance.

Communication for women is a form of intimacy. It deeply affects her soul. She not only needs her husband to talk, but she needs him to listen as well. She wants her conversation taken seriously, and what she says taken into serious consideration. If that does not occur, a husband is going to have a wife who will soon need anger management classes. Either she will become outwardly enraged, or she will withdraw. Both dispositions are unhealthy and dangerous.

A husband can settle his wife's concerns just by listening, considering and communicating with her. Her responsibility is to be an assistant, a helper, a companion. Her thoughts need serious consideration. He need not pacify her with futile agreements. What wife wants her husband to agree just for the sake of agreeing? Would not a husband want his wife to consider things on his behalf?

If the husband contemplated a matter, and his wife caught an oversight, he would want to know, right? Alternatively, would he say, "I want to do it because I said so?" Wow! Silly, maybe even borderline stupid, no? She is a good thing, a wife who is always looking out for her husband's best interest.

Chapter Thirteen

The She-Man

 he intellectual aptitude of a woman is profound. A woman who has become a wife is an incredible asset to her husband. She is a precious jewel, a fine specimen. She has the ability to do anything she chooses and becomes successful and accomplished in her own endeavors. She is capable of reasoning at high levels of conscious.

Some men find her mental aptitude intimidating. She intentionally wants to know a matter in fine detail. She is a communicator and enjoys indulging in conversation. When she is communicating with her husband, she delights in descriptive conversations that employ more than two or three words. She would prefer to hear at least an audible and intellectual complete account of what she inquires.

A woman or *"she-man"* as I call her is powerful. She can become whatever she perceives. She is capable of being the chief executive officer, managing major corporations of thousands. In the worldwide business arena, she can become the world's greatest financial leader. She can represent great nations and negotiate with diplomats around the world. She can govern and rule a whole society of people as a country's queen.

Women can be police officers: schoolteachers, athletes, authors, poets, astronauts, scientists, doctors, lawyers, judges, while performing the duties of wife and mother. She can achieve anything and develop into anyone she chooses. Nevertheless, when she turns the key to unlock the door to her home, she must respond to God's order.

Position

Scripture teaches the wife to be subject to her own husband. To yield: be accountable for her actions, willing to agree with his leadership. A wife ought to respond to her husband's love, and agree with his authority.

God entrusted the husband with the responsibility of headship over his wife. He should save her from any form of humiliation, protect and defend her. For the sake of order, God positioned the husband as the leader of his family. It by no means implies the husband is more than his wife, although he holds a superior position of responsibility. It is the assembly of God's order for His family. God did not create Eve to assume Adam's responsibilities; He created her to help him with them.

Without order, chaos rules, whether in a home or society. Both husband and wife must recognize God's divine arrangement, and their place in it. His order provides for a peaceful society within the home. When both husband and wife step out of God's order, their society erupts into disarray. Both ought to encourage each in God's principals. Neither ought to attempt to force their spouse's compliance.

God first made Adam in His image and crowned him with glory and honor. The glory of Adam was God. The Glory of man is woman. Man represents the authority of God as ruler and head. God built Eve from Adam's flesh and rib. Eve was Adam's glory. Woman is the glory of man. Yet, God made woman in His image as well as man. Woman glorifies God and her husband. We know according to Scripture; God created male and female in His divine image.

The term "Head" expresses, the next immediate relation sustained. God supports man's natural and spiritual dependence. Man supports his wife's natural and spiritual dependence. He is priest and prophet of his home. The husband does not replace God. He leads and supports his wife in spiritual matters as lead by God. God through His son Jesus Christ sustains her through direct relationship with Him. Man when created first came into direct relations with God. Woman when created from man subsequently came into relations with God. God created man and woman to share a dependence on each other. A husband supplies what his wife lacks, and a wife supplies what the husband lacks. They complete their union. All marital matters come from God.

> *A man should not cover his head. He is God's image and glory. The woman, however, is man's glory. ⁸ Clearly, man wasn't made from woman but woman from man. ⁹ Man wasn't created for woman but woman for man. ¹⁰ Therefore, a woman should wear something on her head to show she is under someone's authority, out of respect for the angels. ¹¹ Yet, as believers in the Lord, women couldn't exist without men and men couldn't exist without women. ¹² As a woman came into existence from a man, so men come into existence by women, but everything comes from God* (1ˢᵗ Corinthian 11:7-12 GW).

Reason for the Uproar

Here is a noteworthy mention. During this time in the Scripture noted above the Christian women of Corinth claimed equality with men. They had taken their stand in a very lively and outspoken manner. "The women were coming forward praying and prophesying in their assemblies with uncovered heads." Praying and prophesying, were not the issues, they rebelled against covering their heads, according to customs. Women's refusal to wear a covering on her head while praying and prophesying in the assemblies expressed insubordination and independence. Paul addressed these issues relating the order of assemblies. (Pulpit Commentary).

A woman's head covering also represented something else. She wore it as a sign of delicacy. It also expressed her natural dependence upon her husband. It signified she was under her husband's authority, leadership, and care. It was not a sign to humiliate her. She wore it as a signature piece, presenting herself as a woman cared for by her husband. In God's original economy of family, the wife naturally depended upon her husband's care.

Unfortunately, time and displacement of God's original idea for woman, wife, and marriage no longer applies for most. Women, whether mother or wife, force themselves to nurture and sustain their own care. If man preserved God's original order, treated women as God instructed, women and wives would have come to understand God's original thought; and women would have learned God's expectation of their care for themselves.

A man cannot divinely lead, passionately love, or care for his wife the way God intended, until he totally submits and surrenders his life to God. Until that happens, she will receive a partial understanding in place of whole meaning. She will live and miss knowing what it means to know the love of her man and husband. God loves woman through the love of a man. Man is God's express representative of His thoughts, noble impulses, pure desires, and sympathy.

Leadership

The forefront is the husband's position. God gave him the position to lead, guide, instruct, and direct his wife and family. He receives his direction through the wisdom of God's Word. He is responsible to seek the counsel of God, calculate, consider, and weigh all things for the good for his house. He carries weighty responsibilities on his shoulders. The welfare of his family constantly set before him. His thoughts are perpetual about the good for his house.

How difficult for a husband to lead a wife who resist his leadership? Lack of leadership exposes a home to a chaotic and unpeaceful environment. If the head decides to walk to the right, does not the body follow? For spouses to move in the same direction the head and body must agree.

Can two people walk together without agreeing on the direction? Amos 3:3 (New Living Translation)

If the head decides to go one-way, and the body decides to go another, does it not pull itself apart? Division stands against union, and a divided house will implode within itself. A house divided against itself will never stand (Mark 3:25). When a wife understands she is the body; the neck, which helps turn the head; she can begin to understand her significance in agreeing.

Dr. J. Vernon McGee says that "Her purpose; she is to be the other half of man. She is to respond to him, to answer to him. A wife is the other part of him, the other half of him. He is only half a man without her. She is to be of the same mind as her husband. She is to agree with him and come into a mutual understanding."

Respond

I enjoy walking through the Garden of Eden, metaphorically of course. We can extract such a vast amount of intelligence from within the first paradise. You find behind the defending Cherubim's lie astonishing and valuable information to develop our understanding of role and responsibility as wife. Here, we can discover the reason for her existence.

The Scripture teaches the man with the *womb* (Eve). God created for the *penile* man (Adam). God said, "He saw that it was not good for man to be alone and subsequently remedied the matter. God took a rib from the penile man He created from the dust of the ground, and built a womb man (woman), specifically fitted, as the penile man's complement.

God removed Adam's rib, refashioned it, improved it with extraordinary enrichments, and returned Adam's rib to him in the form of a woman. What He took from Adam He replaced with something much more spectacular than his rib and flesh.

God designed Eve specifically for him, to complement him. God restored Adam's completeness. When God gave Adam his rib back, He restored him completely again. God gave Eve to Adam as a perfect companion and helpmeet. It always amazes me when I think that God created Adam to resemble Himself. God made Eve to resemble Adam, both perfectly resembling God; fascinating!

God built Eve for a specific duty, to be a companion and helper. Eve was Adam's: copilot, his assistant, his assistant manager, his executive officer, his confidant, lover, and his best friend. Eve was all Adam needed.

Eve had co-authority and co-dominion and ruled alongside Adam. She completed what God saw he needed…a helping hand! She knew the reason for her existence. Eve came alongside Adam to perform her duties as Adam's assistant. She did not need a seven steps, six-week training course on how to become; she was. The woman was equipped with everything Adam needed. She was, "Bad all the way down to the bone!"

Women, who heard "submit" whether from society or sitting on the church pew, find it difficult to swallow. When women understand God's order and what the word means, it is beautiful. Misconceptions and misunderstandings of the God's Word, has robbed women, and wives for years.

I have come to find the word *"submit"* is not a harsh or demanding word. Some teach the word submit means to obey, and do what you are told. Children need telling what to do. "Go here, or sit there." A wife needs her husband's leadership, wisdom, and spiritual direction. God created her with intellect. She has a brilliant mind. Her husband ought never to underestimate her ability.

The word "submit" in Ephesians 5:22 is not actually in the Greek text. The interpreters added the word for ease of read. However, the definition of the word is not consistent with the definition of "submit" in Ephesians 5:21. This particular definition in verse 22 is a Greek military term meaning "to arrange [troop divisions] in a military fashion under the command of a leader."

Verse 21 means to agree, to yield, not cause dissention, and to prefer others above self. Regarding husband and wife, it is a tender submission or response to the love of the husband. Her responsibility is to respond to her own husband's love, as she would respond or submit to the love of the Lord; just as the church (the body of Christ), responds to the love of God openly displayed in Christ.

The words submit is a sweet, passionate, and romantic word, it infers the desire of the loved, to surrender to the passion of the faithful lover. It means to yield, agreement, and to place *self* under loving and tender leadership. "*Submit* is a very mild word. It is a loving word. It means to respond to your own husband as you would respond to the love of the Lord. The way we respond to the Lord is that we love Him because He first loved us." –J. Vernon McGee

*21Out of respect for Christ, be courteously reverent to one another. **24** Now as the church submits to Christ,*

so wives are to [submit] to their husbands in everything.
Ephesians 5: 21 & 24 (MSG)

The wife voluntarily submits, yields, or responds to the love and devotion of her husband. The husband ought to resemble Christ in love…so her response will be as unto the Lord. The Lord's love is safe. Her husband's love must represent to her, his safety. She cannot respond or agree to a contradicting love of God, a love contrary to the love of Christ. When he loves as Christ, he will own her response.

Let me stop for a moment and make something perfectly clear. I am not implying or suggesting a man pull out his spine. Negative! A man is the leader, head and authority of his home. However, leadership, authority, and pride, can interfere with providing a wife with the essentials God instructed a husband to submit. While leading, lead with remembering to love.

A Story of Exception

Scripture teaches a wife to place herself under her husband's leadership in everything. As long as the husband follows Christ, which is his Head, she follows him. However, her following ceases when against her own conscious. She is not to submit or agree with what is against the Word of God; God holds her accountable for her obedience or disobedience to Him.

Every man owns his sin and is responsible to God for them. If he is a foolish man, she cannot yield to senseless leadership. If his leadership endangers or threatens her life, she is to use Godly wisdom to save herself from harm. God did not remove a wife's intelligence, wisdom, or understanding. He did not tell her to dummy down, lie down, and act as though she is irrelevant. Her instruction is to agree, and that agreement is with sound counsel from her husband

Do you remember the story of Abigail? Or, recall the story of David running for his life, and hiding in the wilderness? David heard of a wealthy man named Nabal sheering his sheep. Therefore, David sent men, in his name (David's), to greet Nabal, and ask for supplies. He asked, Nabal to give him and his men whatever he could afford.

David hoped his faithfulness would grant a favorable response from Nabal. Since he did not harass or seize anything from his shepherds. Nabal disrespectfully refused David's request. When David heard of Nabal treatment of his men, David commanded his men to put on their swords. He and his men set out to kill Nabal and all his servants.

Now, when Abigail, Nabal's wife heard how David's men were treated, she immediately prepared gifts for David. She sent her servants before her with them. She did not tell her husband; she knew the threat to her life.

When Abigail rode out to meet David, she pleaded with him on behalf of her husband and herself. Because of Abigail's plea, David withdrew from his pursuit of Nabal. Scripture says Abigail was an *intelligent* and *beautiful* woman. Had she agreed with her husband's foolishness her story would read differently.

David told her, "Blessed is your astuteness, and blessed are you as well. This day you kept me from taking part in bloodshed and revenging myself by my own hand. If you had not come to meet me as quickly as you did, your husband Nabal would not have a single man left standing by the time the sun rose" (1st Samuel 25:1-43).

As previously mentioned, the story is an exception, not the rule. However, if there should arise an occasion where you must protect your husband and preserve your life. Defend your home with your God given wisdom and intelligence. I have not seen it written in Scripture that if a husband fails to protect his wife's life, she cannot protect her own.

Women must understand how powerful they are. When God sculpted woman, He equipped her with the ability to do anything. Eve is Adam's rib, stretched out, multiplied, and enriched. Eve possessed what was in Adam. Women are an incredible wonder. God created a he-man and formed a she-man from the man He had created, how marvelous.

God created them equal in power and authority. There will be those who will disagree, however; Scripture teaches that God said, "Let us make man in our image, after our likeness and let *them* have dominion. The key word in this verse is *them*.

Let them have dominion. The plurality of the word *them* refers to both Adam and Eve. Some scholars' say *them* speaks of a forthcoming generation of man. I agree with that position as well, however; I do not believe it is a singular word reserved to future Adam's alone. God made Eve to be a helper to Adam. Without Eve, men could never come forth.

God created Adam as ruler and gave him dominion over everything. God built Eve for Adam, and, as Adam's help. Eve acted as a contributor to further man. Without Eve, man would exist as one living human. She aided Adam in being responsible to obey God's command, to rule and subdue everything. She had co-rule and co-dominion by institution of God's blessing.

In the Pulpit Commentary, Luther sees an indirect suggestion, "that the woman was also created by God and made a partaker of the Divine image, and dominion over all." Adam did not exercise dominion over Eve prior to the fall. They coexisted in divine union. Everything they did was natural and normal. Adam and Eve walked in divine agreement without any counseling sessions. They lived as one, and fell as one from their divine nature. Adam and Eve were the epitome of unity.

God blessed both Adam and Eve and gave them the responsibility to rule. Eve stood by Adam's side ruling with him and making all things subject to them. When God created them, He blessed "*them*" to subdue, and rule over everything.

*Then God said, "Let Us make man in Our image, according to Our likeness; and let **them** rule over the fish of the sea and over the birds of the sky and over the cattle and over all the earth, and over every creeping thing that creeps on the earth." **27** God created man in His own image, in the image of God, He created him; male and female He created **them.28.** God blessed **them**; and God said to **them**, "Be fruitful and multiply, and fill the earth, and subdue it; and rule over the fish of the sea and over the birds of the sky and over every living thing that moves on the earth."* Genesis 1:26-28 (New American Standard Bible)

Resistance

By now, you ought to ascertain Eve's place and position. Do not start cheering so quickly. I hope that these paragraphs will also help you understand, why some women who become wives are full of resistance. I said some, not all. Nevertheless, all can grasp an understanding, clarifying minds.

Let us go back into the Garden again. What did God say to Eve after she gave Adam the fruit? God told Eve, 'your desire will be for your husband and he shall have rule over you.' She did well until she gave Adam that piece of fruit. The results of disobedience cost Eve her freedom, as she knew it.

Eve walked next to her husband with dominion, rule, and authority. God repositioned Eve's authority when she disobeyed Him. Her rule became her husbands'. God did not remove her authority; God simply said, 'you will not use your power as you used to; your husband will rule over your rulership.'

However, your desire and craving will be for your husband, and he will rule over you (Genesis 3:16 (Amplified Bible).

When Eve, a she-man, the counterpart of Adam, sinned; she was sentenced to 'yield' her will to her husband, to "turn" it over to him. She was to put herself under his leadership, subjecting herself to him. Eve was subordinate to Adam in the sense he was the first created by God's hands, but she was not in subjection to him.

God created them with equal rights and blessed them with dominion, and rule. Their agreement formed as natural as a sunrise or sunset. Eve's will agreed with Adam's. She united with him, without thought or consideration. She moved with him in harmony, as a vapor moves when brushed with a stroke of wind, effortlessly.

At the entrance of sin, her liberty and rule as an equal partner reduced, and subjection became punishment. Her submission was no longer, by natural and divine order, but now, by God's adjudication to sin. Adam and Eve lived harmoniously, until sin interrupted their divine state of agreement.

This is interesting because, God did not remove her rule in the sense of making her powerless. He did not shut it down; He did not turn it off. He left it intact, in full force, and operational within her.

This would become every woman's greatest struggle to regain power. If a wife, "Are you always attempting to tell your husband what to do?" Do you want me to answer the question? Ok, yes you do! Woman can lead and govern. That is why when a man steps out of order, abandons his home, and abandons his wife and children. She can pick up where he left off. She ought not to, but when pushed, she will; women are capable.

The fetus-carrying male, or what I call a "she-man," still yearns for the liberty she was accustomed to in the Garden. Interestingly, it is not as if she does not have any liberty. Her liberality is through her husband. Depending on the generosity of her husband's love, and his confidence in her, she can enjoy much liberty. However, if her husband harbors pride, jealousy, selfishness, loveless, and uncharitable, she will not know liberty, only limits.

The nature of a she-man conflicts with God's order. At times, that nature wants to rule. The she-man must come to terms with God's order of arrangement, and stand down. She is not the head or leader in marriage; her husband is. She must bridle her authority and submit her rule over to her husband, and allow him to be the responsible man God chose him to be.

She must understand she is full of power, authority, and dominion; and is co-ruler, not the ruler of the house. That rule belongs to her husband, and she must respect and honor the position of responsibility charged to him by God. Interestingly, when the husband knows his wife honors and respects him, he returns the wife's authority to her. If not careful, he can return too much responsibility to her hurt.

Often when a husband trust his wife, he becomes comfortable with resigning responsibilities. Some of those responsibilities belong to him, and he should not relieve himself of them and give them to her for oversight. They do not belong to her; there are his duties as a husband.

Authority may be returned from the husband. If he returns too much, the wife is overburdened with excessive duties. Duties that, the husband should retain. She is to help him, not necessarily do everything for him. A woman is capable, but what he is accountable for, he ought to carry that weight of responsibility. The wife is not to assume them for him; she is to help. God gave him the fortitude to carry the weight.

A woman or wife can use her power and dominion in the workforce, hallelujah! However, when she comes home, leave power and dominion in the parking lot, garage, or outside the door. I say this, because you as a she-man must understand the attitude, ability, strength, and power working within you as a womb-man. You must remember; from out of man, you came forth. Everything in Adam's bone, his blood, flesh, and DNA move throughout your being. You are as He is, but with divine altercations, constructed by the hand of God.

Adam's physical frame emerged up from the dust as God's creative Spirit formed dust particles into man. God did not return to the dust for woman. God put man to sleep, opened his side, took his flesh and rib, and built woman from them. God adjusted, critiqued, enhanced, enriched, and built woman to assimilate to the one from which she came. There is no other species compatible for man, except woman. Women are spectacular, powerful, and dynamic!

When you understand how powerful you really are; she-man, you must allow, let, and give your husband opportunity to bear the position God confirmed him to occupy. I know it takes self-control to bridle such enormous power. Yet, you must learn to seize your own authority, allowing your husband to assume his God given responsibilities.

If you do not learn, you will cause your husband to perceive he can do nothing for you, as you operate in your authoritative spirit. You can take this for what it is worth. "You never want your husband to believe you have no need of him; or that he is not necessary; or that you can do whatever you need to on your own."

You probably can, but you better not give him any cause to believe he can do nothing for you. Again, take it for what it is worth. Suzie is at work telling him of how wonderful and useful he is. I am not saying, "It is right." I am just giving you something to ponder over. A man yearns to know he is necessary.

Just, as God placed in woman to crave for love; he placed in man to crave for praise; adoration; accolades, and honor. You can stand up as tall as you choose. However, if you do not stand down she-man, he perceives you, his wife as a threat to his self-confidence, affecting his perception of self.

A man adores the respect of his wife. Consider your attempts to participate in what God did not assign to you. Help him, he needs you; stand with him; by his side, aid him; but do not overthrow him!

I hope women can begin to understand some of their frustrations. Hopefully, women can detect why at times she feels the urging to rise up. Stand down she-man, and let God direct all that power, so your house may be in order, and your *soul* at peace (*mind, will,* and *emotional soundness*).

Let your husband handle what God has given him responsibility to shoulder. Yes, you must *let*, allow, step back, and stand down. God made him capable of carrying the burden of leadership. You can lead; it is just that God did not tell you to. Stop trying to be responsible for something God resigned from you. Help him; stop trying to move him out of his place and become him. You move yourself out of order.

Thirsty Desire to Crave

Did you notice the first portion of that aforementioned verse? "Your desire shall be for your husband." The word *desire* is intense. It means: to long after, violently crave, thirst for, greatly desire, run to, and delight in, hunger after. It means to desperately want for your husband. It does not necessarily mean, or refer to a sexual desire either, but a fervent want and strong appetite for him.

God gave wives a passion to hunger for and long for their husbands. This hunger, this crave was a part of Eve's penalty, passed through generations. It is so important for women to understand this desire in them. It is equally important women learn and understand how to master it. A woman will become domineering and out of control, if not.

A husband desires the love of his wife, but not to the point of smothering him. Overbearing passions snuffs his liberty to be himself. Do not oppress him for the sake of love. Do not try to bind him to your hip! Do not try to control his every move. You might be dealing with the deception issue, which occurred, in the Garden.

Women inherited caution and suspicion through Eve understanding deceptive tactics. An invaluable lesson learned from experience and passed through generations. However, you must give your husband some leeway. A man can hardly stand his wife shutting him down. Not able to move, or do anything; watching him like a hound dog. He is not in prison.

You cannot handicap the man. If he goes outside, there you are. If he comes inside, there you are. If he goes in the bathroom, knock, knock, knock you are tapping on the door, "How long are you going to be in there." Maybe in the bathroom he finds peace, or a moment alone to gather his thoughts. Here you are knocking on the door.

You need to learn how to master your emotions. If he cannot move about his home freely; enjoy his liberty; relax and let his hair down, so to speak. He will probably be a workaholic; a husband that you hardly see. He may love you, but he cannot freely breathe and have peace when he is around you. Learn how to control your crave.

Fortunately, God works everything out for the benefit of His people. He has implemented a sweet order of submission predicated on love. The wife submits to her husband; the husband submits to Christ, and Christ submits to God. It is a divine order based on a passionate and love relationship. The wife responds to the love of her husband. The husband responds to the love of Christ, and Christ responds to the love of God. What an awesome love affair!

Independents

There is nothing wrong with women being independent. Women should educate themselves. They ought to know and understanding how to stand on their feet. Especially, after men refused to stand up on their own. A woman cannot sit idly by waiting on prince charming. It is imperative she know how to care for herself.

When you become a man's wife? You must understand the responsibility and role of a companion. Women, who look forward to marriage, ought to study the duties and responsibilities of a wife. Those expectations vary by the desire of the husband. You can run the world, perform, and function in a capacity of excellence. However, when your key clicks the door open, leave the world outside and let your husband be responsible for what God gave him dominion over.

Most of the time when you surrender your authority to your husband, he gives it right back anyway, because he has need of you. He needs his copilot, personal assistant, executive officer. He needs every embellishment God formed in you for him. However, know what they are, and study how to use them in wisdom.

I have found that some independent wives conflict with themselves. They lose the desire to care for and help their husbands. The wife becomes independent of him, however; he remains dependent of her. He retains his dependence and expectation of her support. Some independents frustrate easily.

An independent woman fails to understand certain matters. She falsely expects her husband to function at her level. She multi-tasks extremely well, while her husband still asks for everything. She can do fifty things at one time. Unfortunately, hubby's wiring only connects to five things at once. Independents desire less requested of them. They want their husbands to ask less and do more. Their attitude is; I work just as you do!

Independents want their husbands to articulate and move about life as well as they do. If he does not, she cannot understand why. She cannot fathom why he cannot cook and clean the house. Balance a checkbook, take care of the kids, promote for higher pay. Plan a vacation, pick up his clothes, or pick up his plate, pick up his socks, fix the bed, and take out the trash all in one day. He is not multi-tasked. God did not embellish him with those exceptional traits. You are the help!

When God put man to sleep and took out his rib, God fashioned the woman into someone spectacular. Adam had no concept as to the generosity of his counterpart. God build her from man, and she possessed everything in Adam. Eve was Adam in, she form; modified and improved; the same, yet perfect in difference. She had all his qualities, except physical stamina.

She possessed the ability to articulate thought and reason. God enabled her to calculate, weigh, and independently decide. God incorporated details in Eve that were not fashioned into Adam. God created Eve with compelling complexities. Women consist of elaborate features that still baffle their counterpart today.

However, as I previously mentioned, He did not equip her with equal physical strength. He made her a woman, a more delicate and precious vessel. She was the last thing God made with His hands. He saved the best for last. God assembled Eve carefully and meticulously. She was and is a *good* thing.

Interestingly, God created woman to help man. The man needed help. Wives figure it out. Husbands really need your aid. The additional accessories God added to the woman strengthen her husband's hands. God enriched women with all the extras to complement him well. The wife is the perfect partner.

However, we have become so independent that we do not want our husbands to tell, or sometimes even suggest to us, what to do, let alone, him ask us for help. Any task is undesired. We think we are grown. We make our own money, and we chart our own course. That is true. Nevertheless, ask yourself, does honor live in your house?

As a wife, we can choose God's way or our way. If we choose God's, it calls for a higher order. God's order creates a divine union. What wife wants contention with her husband? What husband loves a wife who refuses to honor him? God's way is not as complicated as spouses make it. What creates a divide is self-seeking spouses who want everything their way. Husbands and wives who choose not to place each other above self; spouses who forget to respect and esteem the other; spouses who fail to love; and spouses who forget to remember God's divine arrangement.

Blue Letter Bible. "Dictionary and Word Search for *hypotassō (Strong's 5293)."* Blue Letter Bible. 1996-2011. 23 Jun 2011.

Chapter Fourteen

Marriage – The Prototype of Christ and the Church

Drastic changes have occurred in the hearts and minds of man. When I refer to man, I mean both male and female. Man as God's created beings reflecting His image in the earth. Some prescribe to the notion of man originating from apes, or other organisms. I am talking about man created by the hand of God.

If you choose to believe man through time, evolved from one species to another, it is your prerogative. To lay the foundation of this message; I believe God created human life, male and female, in His image. Male and female He designed for unity in marriage.

It appears as though men and women misplaced the fundamental precepts and meaning of marriage. Respect for marriage has a lost value. Many men and women, married or single do not respect marriage. Men cheat on their wives; wives cheat on their husbands. Both find little regard for the consequences of their choice.

The children, as well as, the uninvolved parties are heartbroken due to selfish conduct. Standing before God and man esteemed both husband and wife to an honorable position. To exchange vows meant a lifetime commitment. The most important single event a man or woman would achieve in their life. It was a thrill to find your spouse. People used to believe in marriage.

Today women refuse the proposal to wed, and men refuse the proposal to ask. Their thought is, "Why should I? Marriage is a headache." For them to consider walking down the aisle and saying, "I do" is an unappealing prospect. However, male and female desire the benefits, absent the commitment of a vow.

Men and women, inside and outside the church, believers, and unbelievers require understanding. They ought to understand what forms a marriage according to Scripture. Many care less about Scripture's teaching. Fortunately, God granted all the power of choice. God graced everyone with the power to choose his or her influence.

Adam

God created a man with seed to flow from his genitalia. God built woman's womb to receive man's seed. The womb promotes development of the seed into a fetus. The fetus becomes a child and pro-creation continues. Without seed and womb, humanity ends.

God put Adam into a deep sleep, took a rib from him, and fashioned it into a woman. 'Luther inclines to think that Adam's language in Genesis 2 ver. 23 implies that not the bare rib, but the rib with the accompanying flesh was extracted.'

This is the first account of a human surgery. The hand of God performed this procedure. I would estimate that anesthesiologist and surgeons mimicked God's idea. They took God's original idea of inducing deep sleep, causing the physical body's unconsciousness, which provided an opportunity to perform surgeries. However, this they cannot duplicate, performing a surgery without the patient ever feeling pain.

When God put Adam to sleep and removed his rib, God closed up the entry, and when Adam awoke, he did not need Morphine, Oxycontin, Ibuprofen, or Codeine #3. Adam woke to a missing rib. Yet, he incurred no effects of pain.

In order to understand marriage, we need to talk with the one who created it. Otherwise, we form our own ideology. God did not bring Eve to Adam as his woman; God brought her to him as his wife. God gave Eve a divine presentation. When Adam's eyes beheld her sumptuous perfection, he was amazed, excited, and ecstatic to see his own resemblance, a creature just like him in "*she form.*" He immediately recognized her relation to himself. In total astonishment, he declares, "Finally someone who is like me." Adam attracted to Eve instantly.

The Ceremony

God performed the first wedding ceremony in the Garden of Eden. The first account of marriage is of Adam and Eve. Imagine the flourished surroundings. Talk about a garden wedding, this was the epitome of a lush and romantic setting. They were the first to experience such a stunning and flourishing venue designed by the imagination of God.

After forming Eve, God brought her to Adam as his wife. Not only did God the Father give His daughter away in marriage, as a father does, He also gave her to a prepared husband, one who understood the concept of work and responsibility.

God gave Adam the duty, and task to work and take care of his home. God employed the first man to work. Adam had the responsibility to manage and cultivate his living quarters (Genesis 2:15). Did Adam have to work, probably not! God could have cared for the Garden Himself, since He created it, and sustains all things. However, God saw it fitting to give Adam responsibilities, and make him accountable for his divine home.

> *The woman was the last of God's creative works; presumably, therefore, she was the best. "Eve's being made after Adam puts an honor upon that sex as the glory of the man (1 Cor. 11:7) If man is the head, she is the crown-a crown to her husband, the crown of the visible creation. The woman was not made until everything was in the highest state of readiness for her reception. Before her creation, not only must there be a home for her reception, provision for her maintenance, and servants to attend upon her bidding; there must, likewise, be a husband who feels the need of her sweet society, that longs for her coming, and that can appreciate her worth. Hence, he who seeks a partner should first find a house in which to lodge her, the means to support her, but especially the love wherewith to cherish her. Woman was formed out of a finer and more precious material than man, being constructed of a rib taken from his side. "The man was dust refined, but the woman was dust double refined; one remove further from the earth." This was not because of any supposed excellence residing in the matter of a human body. It was designed to indicate woman's unity with man as part of himself, and woman's claim upon man for affection and protection." - Matthew Henry*

Relationship

The union between a husband and wife symbolizes the relationship between Christ and His bride, the church, the people of God. It is a spiritual pattern in the earth, reflecting divine relationship in God's Kingdom. A husband symbolizes Christ, the head of the church. A wife symbolizes the church, the body of Christ. The husband and wife represent a spiritual union, in the physical realm. As Christ and His relationship with the church, glorify God, so does the relations between a husband and wife. Marriage characterizes Christ and His body.

Scripture teaches that Christ loved His church and died to redeem her. A husband is to love his wife in the same way. A husband represents who Christ is and what He gave. Christ gave His life on a silver platter, because of love. Likewise, a husband should openly display his love and passion.

Christ desires a deeper revelation, purity, holiness, and relationship with God for His body. The husband's desire should reflect Christ regarding these things as well. As Christ gave His life for the church, so ought the husband for his wife.

This means that the husband sets aside his own interest to care for and invest in his wife. His investment should cherish and nourish her with not only physical needs, but more importantly, to nourish her in the Word of God, which is essential to her spiritual growth and knowledge of God.

He should encourage her to develop her own intimate and personal relationship with God through Christ Jesus. He should invest time to teach her God's principles, and ideas. He should pray for her and with her.

The husband need not do these things because his wife is incapable of understanding God's Word. She is able to understand. God will define and clarify His Word to her as well as expound and reveal His Word to her husband. However, he is priest and prophet. He assumes the leadership role in his family to teach his house God's Word.

He is to teach in love as Christ teaches in love and is the expression of that very love taught. Thereby, presenting a wife of splendor unto himself, just as Christ would present His body to Himself, whole, healthy, without blemish, and blameless.

When a husband looks upon his wife, he should see a reflection of himself. That reflection should imitate the image of Jesus Christ. A husband ought to see himself in his wife.

God sees us, far beyond the physical features. He can identify His Son, Jesus Christ in us. We are God's because He can see Himself in us. Through His son who lives in all who have accepted Christ as Lord and Savior, God identifies His children. Husband and wife are one, as Christ and His body are one. This is a spiritual unity!

The Scripture further instructs a husband is to love his wife as his own body. The husband is the head, and his wife is his body. Head and body are one! The husband is to love his own wife as he would love his own flesh, for she is as his flesh.

Would he not wash and clean his body? Nourish, preserve, and sustain the health of it? Yes. He would protect his body from hurt and harm. In the face of danger, he would defend it. For what man hates his flesh? He does not; he cares for and nourishes it?

Christ washes, nourishes, sustains, protects, and defends His body. So ought the husband do likewise for his wife, love her as himself. Head and body are not separate; they are one complete unit. Jesus Christ has cleansed His body by the washing of water and by His Word, that He may present His body blameless to Himself.

> *25-28Husbands, go all out in your love for your wives, exactly as Christ did for the church—a love marked by giving, not getting. Christ's love makes the church whole. His words evoke her beauty. Everything he does and says is designed to bring the best out of her, dressing her in dazzling white silk, radiant with holiness. And that is how husbands ought to love their wives. They're really doing themselves a favor— since they're already "one" in marriage.*

> *29-33No one abuses his own body, does he? No, he feeds and pampers it. That's how Christ treats us, the church, since we are part of his body. And this is why a man leaves father and mother and cherishes his wife. No longer two,*

they become "one flesh." This is a huge mystery, and I don't pretend to understand it all. What is clearest to me is the way Christ treats the church. And this provides a good picture of how each husband is to treat his wife, loving himself in loving her, and how each wife is to honor her husband (Ephesians 5:25-31 MSG).

"Scripture taken from *The Message*. Copyright © 1993, 1994, 1995, 1996, 2000, 2001, 2002. Used by permission of NavPress Publishing Group."

Chapter Fifteen

Communication

*E*ffective communication is a learned skill, and a great asset in marriage. When husband and wife can effectively talk, their responses appeal to the heart. Communication is hard, when neither husband nor wife know how to talk to each other, or want to talk for that matter. It requires one person to speak while the other person listens. This means listening without preparing a defense.

Ineffective communication typically occurs when either spouse raises a complaint about the other. Defense mechanisms rise to the surface. While one-spouse talks, the other interrupts, or intrudes defending themselves. Our natural response wants to stand in defense of what we hear. Especially when a spouse points out a wrong, either husband or wife has done.

The concerned spouse cares nothing about a defense. Actually, standing in defense of self only adds fuel to the fire. A spouse wants their husband or wife to listen to their concern with an opened ear and heart. Not defend self, but rather to acknowledge the wrong, and take responsibility for the error. A husband or wife wants an answer to the issue, not a defense for the issue. They seek a resolution to resolve the issue and put it behind them.

When both spouses talk, that means no one is listening. Neither listens to resolve the concern, because someone became offended. Spouses restrict each other's open, honest, and candid, conversations when feelings bruise. They tend to respond through hurt emotions instead of constructively listening to the issue.

Hurt feelings need control. Otherwise, instead of engaging in mature conversations, spouses engage in mudslinging fights. Each spouse throws past faults into the current issue, because of offenses. An attempt to resolve the concern becomes misconstrued. The reason for initiating the conversation ends meaningless. However, the issue, concern, or matters still exist.

Whether acknowledging it or not, spouses sabotage each other's concerns. The issue of the concerning spouse remains unresolved. The concern lingers waiting to return. Often, returning fueled with frustration and aggression. The unresolved matter brews, an incident, a trouble, another dislike triggers its eruption.

Any issue set on the table needs resolution, great or small. Spouses will engage in conversations and end conversations without getting to the bottom line. Concluding a conversation without concluding its issue is haunting. Haunting, as the issue nibbles away at a spouse's peace. Their concern goes invalidated.

If the issue does not affect the marriage and tranquility in the home, do not trip. For instance, if a husband wants to go to the movies and the wife does not. Husbands go to the movies, and vise a versa. Some spouses want control over their husbands or wife's every movement. God have mercy!

There is liberty in marriage, as long as spouses use their liberty responsibly, respectfully, and with their husband or wife in mind. The key thought is this: when your spouse is with you, how do you act? Alone or with friends, act the same way as if your spouse was by your side. Your spouse is with you. You two are one; remember that! Represent your other half respectfully.

Now, spouses do not agree on every iota. Husband and wife can find themselves unable to reach an agreement, due to differences of opinion. However, they can agree to disagree respectively. The reality is this: you must consider the impact your decision will make or not make on your marriage. Do not sweat the small stuff, which does not mean anything! Now, if the issue affects your marriages, you better find some common ground, and learn how to shut-up, listen, and compromise. Big issues require much reflection, and often, effective change for sound resolutions.

Conversations can affect a spouse's attitude. When spouses express dislike about their husband or wife, circumstance or situation; the offended flairs up. Anytime a husband addresses his wife, or vice versa, the implications sound disheartening. It triggers embarrassment and shame. Embarrassed spouses not always know how to handle the truth. Therefore, they strike back with dislikes of their own.

It seems to make the offended spouse a little less discomforted when they sling their own mud. Unfortunately, the husband or wife who brought forth the concern brought it forward as an issue to resolve. They did not bring it up to start a mudslinging fight. Yet, pointing fingers makes one feel less guilty about their own wrongs.

If spouses are not careful to listen, instead of react to the complaint, they devalue their husband or wife's concerns. A spouse ought to acknowledge the significance of their husband or wife's interest.

How Do We Listen?

Often, we do not listen and take to heart what our spouse's say. We listen attentively; it seems, but without any real change.

Sometimes we lack genuine concern, and take them for granted. Our disposition reflects a lack of care for their heart and state of mind. When we do not respond with our undivided attention, we hear though the mumble of our distracted minds. Our behavior demonstrates whether we took the matter to heart. If we did, we will accommodate, modify, and change if need be. If not, we do nothing.

Repeatedly trying to seek resolution can break a spouse down. Tiredness and fatigue will promote frustration. Before you know it, frustration takes over; and anger and bitterness wear like a garment.

Regard and consider your husband or wife's concern; acknowledgment them, and work together through a resolution. Give your undivided attention. You can eliminate unnecessary frustration in your marriage; attend to the heart the first time.

Sharing Words

Words are potent! It is how we communicate, whether written, verbally, or through sign language. Communication is powerful. We function and move about the earth communicating. We converse at work, with our families, spouses, and friends. It is the human tool used for understanding. Of the many people, we talk with; our greatest want is for our spouses to communicate and understand us completely.

Everyone wants someone to understand him or her. Typically, the closest person understands everything about you. Husbands and wives want their spouses as that closest person. A natural expectation is that your spouse knows and understands you better than anyone else. Spouses who believe their husband or wife is oblivious to who they are…wants. They want for recognition and understanding.

To live with a spouse who does not understand your concerns is challenging. Husbands and wives make countless efforts trying to communicate their distresses. When a spouse lacks care for the other spouses' concerns, the danger zone is up ahead. A spouse can fill up with frustration when unresolved issues arise. They incline to share their heart with whoever will listen. Listening is important and dangerous when spouses close their ears.

Spouses often share with others, when their own spouses will not listen. They just want someone to hear, to rest their problems, and relieve the pressure. An innocent want to fulfill an innocent need, someone's ear to listen. Unfortunately, the opposite sex frequently lends an ear or two. Someone who the spouse should never share his or her personal affairs.

Communicating your feeling, passions, etc., with the opposite sex is dangerous. Communicating personal concerns with the same sex might become a real life nightmare, as well. Not all esteem marriage. If you share your concerns with an undercover hoochie koochie mama, or a hoochie man, you just opened problems on top of your problems.

A few words can spark an affair with the discontented. An affair landing between a pair of hotel sheets, or a lovers' bedroom all begins with just a few words. Indiscretions begin with communicating. A conversation, a verbal gesture, or some form of message. Communicating to someone what a spouse ought not to tell, say, or do. Words attract many spouses into participating in affairs.

What happens when someone satisfies a husband or wife's void? Spouses want their husband, or wife to listen, and validate their concerns. If not, when discontented, another ear will please them. Especially, when that ear desires to hear, and appears to understand their marital challenges. Friendships develop out of care and consideration for the person's dilemma. Soon ease and comfortableness set the course to continue conveying other personal matters. Void and wanting spouses become more comfortable sharing. Telling what they ought not.

What develops is an intimate relationship though intimate disclosures. These conversations are incubators for infidelity. They nurture and strengthen its development. The more intimate the conversations, the greater its push to birth an affair. Married couples somehow think this is not betrayal. Betrayal may be a strong word; nevertheless, it is what it is. Anytime husband or wife divulges intimate concerns to another; and finds comfort and emotional support; it is an emotional affair.

Spouses share their hearts with others, believing the listener supports what they feel. The benevolent and considerate listener, at first listens faithfully. Soon, listener becomes adviser, and shares their counsel regarding the spouses concerns. Usually, listeners express thoughts about the kind of care the spouse ought to receive. They articulate how they would treat them so much better, if it were their situation.

Attentive to the details; compassion exchanges its cloak for passion; as everything the spouse divulges becomes supported by passionate sensitive words. What began as a few words, ends with the spouse and listener, talking in premeditated places of which either has no business. Fortunately, this will not become everyone's familiar story. However, an unfortunate experience of many.

Many husbands and wives express their concerns to each other extremely well. Resolve their marital issues and move on to the next challenge in their marriage, if any exist. Marriages end in affairs, because a husband or wife failed to responds to the initial concerns of their spouse. Their spouses discovered comfort in communicating their concerns to someone else. The concerned listener's sympathy turns to passion for the spouse. The spouse's feelings stir for the listener, because the listener validates his or her importance.

Marriage is a work in progress. It is a constant progressive move forward, if spouses choose to progress. A spouse, who hears but does not listen, can cause bruising to the heart. Bruises are not always apparent when injuries happen. A spouse may not detect the heart's injury, but he or she feels the hurt.

Intimacy between a husband and wife is crucial. Spiritual intimacy is deeper and greater than sexual intimacy will ever become. Union of soul and mind intertwines two people into living in the same heart. Sexual intimacy becomes the cake's icing with multiple cherries on top. Spiritual intimacy between husband and wife compares to nothing else.

When a husband or wife can see their spouse for who they are, the spouses' soul satisfies. The ability to see is beyond natural sight. Natural sight is confined to natural limits. Husband and wives need spiritual sight to perceive the heart, soul, and mind of their spouse. This kind of understanding requires dedication, communion, and time.

Husband and wives should establish communication as one of their highest priorities. Communication ought to be more than just conversation. Conversation is simple dialogue, everyday chatter, and the exchange of information. Effective communication in marriage is sharing each other's mind and heart, with the intent to hear and listen.

Hear and listen bear similar but different meanings. *Hear* means to pay attention; concentration, perceive by the ear; to learn by the ear or be told; to listen with favor, agreement, or compliance; conforming or yielding, listen, and pay attention. *Listen* means to give an ear; give attention with purpose of paying consideration; heed and obey; hear with intent; pay close attention to. Both meanings need to apply whenever spouses communicate.

Husband and wife ought to want to understanding as well as have themselves understood. Most importantly, husband and wives ought to consider one another genuinely. If one person is affected, the other should want to help. Without listening and hearing, spouses resist giving due consideration. A husband or wife cannot consider what they do not hear.

Learning How to Shut-Up

I believed my communication skills were good. I deemed myself a good listener, and thought I responded appropriately when my turn to speak. One afternoon my husband and I sat around the house enjoying the day. My husband asked if he could talk with me. Eager to hear him, I asked, "What's up babe?" He said, "I want to talk to you, and I don't want you to say a word until I'm finished." He was very sweet and humble in his request. So I said, "Ok!"

He began explaining how I offended him. Five minutes probably passed and I was getting pissed off! I wanted to say something so bad, but I agreed not to say a word. Had I known I was in for a tongue-lashing, I would not have said yes. His discourse caught me unaware. I listened to him assault my character. "Who does he think he is?" Now I thought it, but I did not say it!

I wanted to strike back. I had plenty of arsenal stored up. It took everything in me to keep my mouth shut, as he so eloquently explained my nasty disposition. He let me know how unappreciative he was of my attitude towards him. I could not take it anymore. I made a hand gesture to interrupt him so I could speak. However, he kindly stopped me and said, "This is not about you right now; this is about me, and I need you to listen. When you have an issue with me, you can bring it to my attention. Right now, I need you to listen to what I am saying."

I thought I was already pissed off, but this took me to the outer limits. I was fuming; you could probably see the steam emanating from the top of my head. My pride was bruised; my heart was on the floor. I thought, "Who does he think he is talking to? I do not have to stand here and listen to this."

In the middle of, my temper tantrum, a small voice pierced through my thoughts, "Listen, listen to his heart, he is hurting. He is trying to share his heart with you." Suddenly, seriously, suddenly, my disposition changed, my emotions settled, and I engaged my heart to listen. I silenced my pride, and pushed away my hurt feelings to make room for his words to take effect in my heart. I understood he was not intentionally trying to hurt me. Therefore, I stood there and listened, brokenhearted I listened, with crushed pride I listened, and I listened until he was finished.

He helped me realize my acts of inconsideration. What he conveyed was what I needed to hear to correct my behavior. His words were not easy to swallow, but I managed to ingest them, as I periodically gagged, as they settled in my heart. My conduct needed polishing. I lacked appreciation, spoke in condescending ways, and needed an anger management class. Seriously, I really needed a class.

I walked out with my head down. I was hurt, embarrassed, and saddened; by the way, he described my attitude. I sat in the next room, going over what he said. I thought, "Where have I been? I had better check myself. My husband is beautifully spirited." I chose to refuse to allow my marriage to suffer over a stinky attitude I could correct.

Was it easy to stand there and listen, of course not? I wanted to use my tongue like a baseball bat and hit every word out of the park. I wanted to defend myself. State my illegitimate excuses that carried no bearing. Pinpoint what he did to feel a bit better about my nasty attitude. Argue why I behave so ugly.

If I opened my mouth, I would have argued against the truth. I would have deprived him of the opportunity to heal his hurt. He would have believed his words were meaningless, and counted for nothing. Rather than display love, I would have displayed excuses to stay the same.

Spouses are responsible for their own attitudes. Claiming the person made you act ugly, is a lie. You act ugly because you are ugly. Individuals are guilty for their bad behavior. What is in you is in you. A person can correct that funky disposition, but they must acknowledge it exists first. Arguing your defense moves you further from the truth about yourself.

I ignored the truth because of my hidden justifications. It resulted in unwelcomed behavior toward my husband. My husband found it mandatory to address my disregarding dispositions. He was right to do so! The most crucial thing was I identify the behavior he addressed and take full responsibility for it.

To not stand my ground and fight back word-for-word was a challenge. I knew how to do that well. My first thoughts were to, "Tell him all about what he did!" However, this was not a time for posturing, but for humbling me. I needed to stand before my husband and listen to his heart. Afterwards, I took a deep breath, apologized, and asked for his forgiveness.

I apologized for every single wrong he cited, and asked forgiveness for each wrong. I set my mind against those character flaws, and committed my attitude to change. Every day I allowed his words to resonate. I chose not to forget what he had spoken. I became alert and considered my words and conduct. If I slipped, he would say, "Watch your tone, check yourself."

Thank God, he did not shut down, go inside himself, and give up. It was all by the grace of God. Today, that singular thought still rides through my mind when my husband and I communicate. There are times when I have jumped my turn, and like a slingshot, his words thrust to the forefront of my mind. "Listen, he is talking." I quickly apologized. Why, because I need to listen to what he wants to say. We both realize that if we allow our emotions to govern us, we will never hear or listen to each other with our whole heart.

After all these years, we still work on mastering this skill. At times, we stop and laugh at each other and say, "Who's supposed to be talking right now?" Listening is a conscious consideration; you must remember to give it your diligent effort.

Misunderstandings

Has your spouse ever misunderstood what you said, or misinterpreted your words? Has your spouse repeated what you said? However, what they repeated was not even, close to what you spoke? Husbands and wives can sometimes filter their spouses' words through their mind and transform the whole meaning. By the time their mind evaluates what they heard and releases it out their mouth; you are lost in translation.

You must be careful to clarify every word, because some do not necessarily listen, they translate. It can frustrate, as well as, affect your desire to want to engage in conversation. Occasionally, a husband or wife may wonder with whom am I talking. You look at each other like; who are you? It is discouraging when you talk to your spouse, and they just do not get it. Whatever you say interprets into something you did not speak. You start off knowing and understanding what you said, and by the end of the conversation, you are confused.

Sometimes spouses are just not good listeners. Words filter through emotions, psychological ideologies, ethnic teaching, and experiences. When spouses run each other's words through filters, they are misunderstood. Spouses who decline to listen with an open mind listen through their own views. They hardly every hear what their husband or wife is saying.

Men and women assess words emotionally and psychologically. When they do, they are not truly listening. They listen to what they think their spouse said. This is a difficult conversation to try to engage in. For the most part, it becomes frustrating.

Husband and wives should carefully listen without preconceived notions. They should not read into the words, just listen to the words. Sometimes this is the biggest gap in spouses communicating effectively; misinterpreting what they hear.

A couple of years after marriage, my husband, and I went back and forth trying to understand each other. I would communicate a matter, and he would repeat what he thought I said. I asked him, "Is that what you heard me say?" He would share an issue with me, after I commented, he would say, "That is not what I said, honey."

Usually, we interpret instead of simply listening. My husband and I decided to ask instead of assuming what the other said. It caused us to talk for hours asking question of each other for clarification. It has worked out very well. Sometimes it may be a day or two before we ask, "What did you mean when you said?" However, it gives each of us a wonderful opportunity to explain what we truly meant.

It is wonderful, because when I hear what he thought, it was not what I meant. I am grateful he asks. His asking affords me the opportunity to clarify my comments. He does the same for me. In this way, we stay on the same page. It is so much easier when we understand each other.

Scripture teaches husbands to dwell with their wives with understanding (1st Peter 3:7). Personally, wives ought to learn their husbands as well. When we understand it is easier to move in unity. In order to understand each other, we must learn to communicate. In communicating, we must learn how to listen. Listening requires engaging the full attention of your heart and mind without filters. We simply listen to words spoken as they are.

Give each other the room to grow patiently. If your spouse makes a comment and you lack understanding, respectfully ask your spouse to explain. Make sure you exchange assumptions for clarification, it is always better when you do.

Countenance

Facial expressions and tone will shut a conversation down. I do not care if you are male or female, if you are staring at an ugly twisted face you just want to run. The face resembles your husband or wife, but it appears as if they encountered a hostile alien takeover. You know you love your spouse, but at that moment, you want to save yourself from the alien threat. You do not want to end up looking like them.

Husband and wives ought to glance in a mirror when talking. Just for a quick peek at their facial expressions when communicating. Facial expressions are scary. Spouses need to see what their husband or wife sees. They might stop and ask themselves, "Why do I look so crazy?" "Well, probably while in the moment, you look just like you are acting…crazy."

In a marriage coaching session, the wife said her husband told her, when she spoke, her face appeared contorted. He did not like it. He felt as though he could not talk to her. He could not understand or figure her out. Her facial expressions incapacitated his response. He did not want to communicate.

Women are often so emotional; all a man notices is anger, rage, and frustration. Whatever she says, he typically does not hear. Her alien face speaks louder than the actual words she utters. The more she twists her face, the more he thinks, "I don't understand her, she is crazy; let me get out of here."

A wife really needs to learn how to communicate without the emotional drama. Not to say what she feels is not legitimate. Nevertheless, she must learn how to master her emotions. Women will say anything and act indignant when emotions rule instead of intellect. The heart and mind, not the heart alone must delegate conversations. We learn from Scripture that the heart is not correct. A wife should master her emotions to think clearly. In this way, she can effectively articulate what she wants to say. She can speak with her heart, but govern her heart with her mind.

> *The heart is deceitful above all things, and it is exceedingly perverse and corrupt and severely, mortally sick! Who can know it [perceive, understand, be acquainted with his own heart and mind] (Jeremiah 17:9 AMP)?*

A husband has no problem engaging in conversations, as long as the wife refrains from screaming, shouting, and acting as if she lost her mind. Men are combative by nature. Their nature is to fight and defend. When a woman acts out against her husband, it places him in a defensive posture. She no longer stands by his side; she stands in his face as an attacker. Being a woman, he might shut down. Alternatively, being a man he might defend himself. If he defends himself, he will act as crazy as she does. It does not make it right; I am just telling you what is real.

I read an article titled, "Why You're "Angry Face" Scares Him." In the article, it, 'Turns out there's a scientific reason why some men shut down during an argument (unscientifically known as "staring at you like, *duh*"). A recent study found that stressed men who looked at angry faces had diminished activity in the brain regions responsible for empathy and understanding.

Researchers had men dunk a hand in ice water to raise their stress hormone levels, and then showed them pictures of people with neutral and anger expressions. "When they viewed the angry faces those areas of their brains became less engaged," says study author Mara Mather, Ph.D. "Basically, it becomes hard for them to interpret other's emotions." So next time you get mad at him, try to vent without scowl. He'll be less likely to freeze, more likely to listen. -Nicole Yorio

Communication is essential, effective communication is an asset. Learn how to speak without illustrating anger. Furthermore, if your spouse lacks the response you want, do not give up on him or her. Lovingly and kindly, continue to bring forth your concern until both of you find a resolution. Your attempts may become frustrating but do not give up. Cease from sharing with the opposite gender. Your intimate affairs are no one else's business; except you and your spouse.

Conclusion

When all said and done. What kind of relationships do we promote? Do we act upon what we know is best for the other, or have we become so selfish we live disregarding. Traditions cause both men and women to participate in backward thinking. Therefore, each thinks at a level of conscience inconsistent with God's idea.

In order for marriage to thrive, both man and woman must know what God said, not what they think God said. Nor can marriages continue to embrace traditions, which teach and reflect negative dispositions. How many of us really sought Scripture, to find biblical truth, regarding relations between man and woman, or husband and wife? We did not! We simply listened to what we were told, and adopted the ideologies of what the people before us instituted.

It has never been God's intention for man to mistreat woman. Somehow, we all have been turned and twisted by tradition, religion, and the idea that if my father did it so I will; or if my mother did it this way, I will also. How many of us, both male and female stopped long enough to say, "God is this Your idea of how we are to interact with one other? If so, then why are we so broken?"

No one can be free living under oppression. I say that to both men and women. Both have the tendency to oppress one another with their own concepts and ideas. When God formed the marital relation, He formed an amazing union between man and woman. He formed something no other persons outside of marriage relations could have. He merged two pieces of flesh into one being. Man does not do this, God does. He blended a unity to last until death. How many of us learned how to maintain, sustain, and nurture what God gave us? It is not incumbent upon God to do this; we must choose to obligate ourselves to know His ways. He gave us the keys, and formulas.

Sadly, we do not look at God's way. We prefer to look to our own. In addition, those who do look to God walk away from Him still authoring their own perspectives. Evidently, some of us want change, and some of us do not. For those who desire a much healthier union, you must go back to the drawing board. The current board has too much chalk residue. We cannot see or define the writing, until we wash the debris from our minds and refresh it with the Word of the true and living God.

Some may resent what is between these pages. They will contend it is something to cause a stir. If it stirs the heart of one man and women to look again and rethink God's way, then I have accomplished my task. I hope that they will find a way to the sweet nectar, and taste the flavor of marriage, the way God intended.

FROM THE FATHER'S HEART

A situational poetic glimpse into relationship with God

ISBN 978-1-61739-022-7

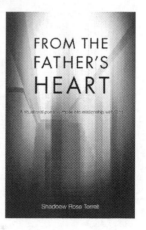

From the Father's Heart is a wonderful reality of intercourse with God through the affairs of one who believes Him. The author's real life situations and circumstances fill the pages only to reveal God's inspiration in poetic form during each occurrence. From The Father's Heart will not only inspire you, but build your faith in believing God really does hear and answer, when you pray.

For more information on Shadoew Rose, or to obtain additional books, please visit:

www.shadoew.com